American Culinary Federation's Guide to

Culinary Certification

The Mark of Professionalism

American Culinary Federation
Michael Baskette, CEC, CCE, AAC
Brad Barnes, CMC, CCA, AAC

American Culinary Federation
since 1929

WILEY

John Wiley & Sons, Inc.

Published by John Wiley & Sons, Inc., Hoboken, New Jersey
Published simultaneously in Canada

For general information on our other products and services or for technical
support, please contact our Customer Care Department within the United States at
(800) 762-2974, outside the United States at (317) 572-3993 or fax (317) 572-4002.

Wiley also publishes its books in a variety of electronic formats. Some content that
appears in print may not be available in electronic books. For more information
about Wiley products, visit our web site at www.wiley.com.

Library of Congress Cataloging-in-Publication Data:

Baskette, Michael.
    American Culinary Federation's guide to culinary certification : the mark of
professionalism / by Michael Baskette, Brad Barnes.
        p. cm.
    Includes index.
    ISBN-13: 978-0-471-72339-4
    ISBN-10: 0-471-72339-8
    1. Food service—Vocational guidance—United States.   2. Cookery—Vocational
guidance—United States.   I. Barnes, Brad.   II. American Culinary Federation.
III. Title.
TX911.3.V62B37 2006
641.5'023'73—dc22   2005005174

Printed in the United States of America

10 9 8 7 6 5 4 3 2 1

Contents

iii

Contents

Foreword

PROFESSIONAL DEVELOPMENT IS A LIFE-LONG COMMITMENT that thousands of cooks, bakers, and chefs embark on every year. It may begin in the classroom or as an apprentice or on-the-job trainee, but it will continue for many years to come. Continuing study, practice, and testing help one build professional characteristics that last a lifetime.

Certification by the American Culinary Federation (ACF) is not only a mark of professionalism, but it is also a roadmap by which a young culinarian can grow and shape his or her entire career. It has led thousands of culinarians to top culinary positions in the nation, and it can do so for you too.

When I started out as an apprentice many years ago I only dreamed of being an ACF Certified Master Chef, but with perseverance and hard work I made it through the many challenges and obstacles I found along the way. Now I am the executive chef of an exclusive country club in New York, team manager of the ACF Culinary Olympic Team, and ACF national president, and I accomplished all of it just one step at a time.

I'd like to dedicate this book to all the cooks and chefs who have embraced the ACF certification processes and practical tests as true measures of professionalism. These are the cooks and chefs who are proud of their accomplishments every step of the way, and look forward to new challenges with vigor, pride, and hospitality.

EDWARD G. LEONARD, CMC, AAC
ACF National President
WACS Vice President
ACF Culinary Team Manager
Executive Chef Westchester Country Club

Preface

THE AMERICAN CULINARY FEDERATION (ACF) BEGAN ITS PROFESSIONAL CERTIFICATION PROGRAM in 1974 as a way of measuring a cook's or chef's level of competency and matching those competencies to national and international culinary standards. It was the first attempt any organization had made to champion the causes of the American chef and garner for them the professional recognition and courtesies they deserved. Since then the ACF has certified tens of thousands of cooks and chefs and has had its program tested and accepted around the world.

The ACF's certification program and the processes that embody it have evolved over the years to include a variety of certification levels in multiple career tracks including professional cooking, pastries, education, and administration. Each one is based on the same model of foundational knowledge; mandatory study in sanitation, nutrition, and supervision; and the theory that it takes continuous study and progressive experiences to develop success in the complex and diverse foodservice industry.

This book attempts to explain the whole concept of professional development and the many levels of professionalism that a culinarian can achieve along the way. The career development ladder that has become the ACF certification process is the set of benchmarks that almost any active culinarian can aspire to. If one is to successfully map his or her career and measure achievement as a cook or chef, then the system outlined in this book is paramount to conquer. The pages to follow will help you to understand how the system works and how to successfully apply this approach to your career in the food industry. Whether you are just starting out in your culinary career, rounding a corner, or headed for that one big job at last, ACF certification can help you achieve your goals.

The History of ACF Certification

THE FOODSERVICE/HOSPITALITY INDUSTRY IS HIGHLY DIVERSE, comprising many segments and offering a variety of career paths few other industries can match. Restaurants, hotels, clubs, private clubs, catering, corporations, and cruise ships offer just some of the numerous professional opportunities in this far-reaching field. Yet regardless of the type of foodservice/hospitality operation in which a culinarian works, the basic tenets of quality foodservice and hospitality remain the same: to prepare nutritious and delicious food, to handle food safely, and to ensure consistently high-level service. These are common goals shared by cooks and chefs in all facets of foodservice.

The American Culinary Federation (ACF) promotes quality foodservice for all segments of the industry, whether in a deli-café, an independent restaurant, or a five-star resort. Wherever people eat and however much they pay for their meal, the ACF maintains that all food should be presented appropriately and in an appealing manner, to stimulate the customer's appetite and then satisfy that hunger.

1

Such high-quality foodservice can be accomplished only by professionals who strive for perfection, to prepare and serve the best foods possible in every circumstance. Anyone can cook, but few have the passion for food that leads them to gain the expertise of a trained culinarian, someone who can transform the simplest ingredients into the most delectable dishes. In short, quality foodservice can be achieved only when someone has the requisite knowledge, skills, and passion.

To that end, the ACF, founded in New York City in 1929, lists as its mission:

> To make a positive difference for culinarians through education, apprenticeship, and certification, while creating a fraternal bond of respect and integrity among culinarians everywhere.

Now headquartered in St. Augustine, Florida, the ACF accomplishes its mission by hosting regional and national conferences and conventions, where trends and new ideas can be learned and shared; by promoting standards for culinary education in academic and on-the-job training programs; through sponsorship of culinary competitions on regional, national, and international levels; by researching and analyzing national and international trends in cooking and baking, and by passing the information on to its members, associates, and partners; and, finally, by continuing to promote professional cooks and chefs as artisans, leaders, educators, and managers to the American public and to the world at large.

The network of professional cooks and chefs who make up the membership and partners of the ACF reaches across the United States and into the global community. ACF is a member of the World Association of Cooks Societies (WACS), and currently holds that organization's presidium (the representative board of directors for WACS) for a four-year term (2004–2008).

SETTING THE BAR FOR PROFESSIONAL DEVELOPMENT

The career path of the chef in the twenty-first century requires a lifetime of learning, progressive skills development, and professional networking. To serve as guideposts along that long path, the ACF professional cooks and chefs certification program was devised in the early 1970s as a validation process, for three primary purposes:

- To measure the competencies of both cooks and chefs at various stages of their professional development.
- To set a national standard for developing professional chef careers.
- To serve as a means to measure success throughout the process.

At the same time, the ACF began formulating its national apprenticeship program, funded through a federal grant program administered by the U.S. Department of Labor. A critical requirement of that program was that all apprentice instructors had to be certified to teach culinary arts. Few cooks and chefs at that time had graduated from formal culinary schools, so a formalized validation process—taking into consideration education, experience, and dedication to the profession—was necessary to give integrity to all formal culinary education programs.

In acknowledgment of that necessity, the ACF developed its first certification program in the early 1970s under the guidance of Johannes Verdonkschot, CEC, AAC, who was then executive chef of the famous Missouri Athletic Club in St. Louis, Missouri, and chair of the newly appointed Committee for Certification of Executive Chefs under ACF president Jack Sullivan's administration (1967–1973). That first attempt to certify culinary ability was limited to the executive chef level only, though it quickly became evident that, for the program to gain national acceptance, it would have to become a measurable and obtainable process that evaluated a professional's entire portfolio of skills.

Taking up the challenge to devise a national certification program for cooks and chefs that would measure successes, test competencies, and require continuing education for a lifetime of career development were three pioneering chefs: L. Edwin Brown, an instructor at the Boyce Campus of the Community College of Allegheny County, Pittsburgh, Pennsylvania (who later became the ACF executive director from 1980–1994); Ferdinand Metz (at the time working as a research chef for

3

Heinz Corporation in Pittsburgh, Pennsylvania, before taking the position of president of the Culinary Institute of America, and later ACF's twelfth national president); and Jack Braun, a Pittsburgh restaurateur (who would become ACF's fourteenth national president).

The three chefs began by researching existing certification programs from other national agencies. In particular, they studied national organizations such as the Dietary Managers' Association, the American Hotel and Motel Association, and the Club Managers' Association, which already had successful certification programs. By comparing the guidelines from each of those programs, Brown, Metz, and Braun were able to build a framework for culinary certifications based on the same overriding principles.

The basis of certification for all three agencies included formal and informal education, measurable competencies, testing, and continuing education as a requisite for maintaining already earned certifications. The ACF certification "ladder," initially composed of five levels, was successfully launched at the ACF 1973 National Convention in Miami, Florida. These levels were:

- Certified Apprentice
- Certified Cook
- Certified Working Chef
- Certified Executive Chef
- Certified Master Chef

Baking and pastry parallel certifications were also created at the same time. Other certification levels such as Culinary Educator soon followed.

GAINING DISTINCTION

As late as the middle of the 1970s, the U.S. Department of Labor in its highly regarded *Dictionary of Occupational Titles* classified the positions of cook and chef as "domestics," alongside household cooks, maids, and chauffeurs. This misnomer went largely unnoticed by most culinarians, who were too busy working their way up their career ladder to pay attention to occupational listings. But as the concepts of professional development for cooks and chefs began to take shape, thanks to the development and implementation of the ACF apprenticeship and certification programs, the definition of "chef" as a distinct occupation began to take entirely new form.

But it took the focused efforts of one man, Louis I. Szathmary, the famous chef-owner of The Bakery in Chicago, Illinois, to make the occupational break from "domestic" complete and final. It was at the 1974 ACF National Convention in Cleveland, Ohio, that Chef Szathmary implored the members of the American Culinary Federation to lead a brigade to Washington, D.C., to have the occupational category of "chef" made separate and distinct. With his now-famous speech, "Greeting Fellow Domestics," Szathmary had the delegates on their feet, inspiring them with hope and drive.

Szathmary (1919–1996) was a nontraditionalist chef who earned a doctorate in psychology from the University of Budapest, Hungary, in 1944 before deciding to pursue a career as a professional chef and restaurateur. But it wasn't until he emigrated to the United States in 1951 that he would find success in his chosen field. Chef Szathmary worked hard to build a reputation for himself and the fine food he served at The Bakery, the restaurant he opened in the Windy City in 1962. In both efforts he succeeded admirably.

Two who were later impressed by Szathmary were in the audience when he gave his enlightened speech in 1974: Dr. Lewis J. Minor, founder of the L.J. Minor Corporation, a national soup and sauce base company, and retired Army Lieutenant General John McLaughlin, who had recently taken over as CEO and president of the Minor Corporation. They decided to join forces with Szathmary, and together they launched a political campaign that would change the status of the American chef forever.

It took two years of determination, research, intense interviewing, and lobbying to convince the federal government, but finally, at the 1976 ACF National Convention, General McLaughlin was able to announce that they had succeeded in convincing the U.S. Department of Labor to officially recognize the American cook and chef as a professional occupational category.

5

THE NEW PROFESSIONAL CHEF

The roles and responsibilities of the cook and chef have been evolving continually since the earliest culinary practitioners donned their aprons. In particular, in the late nineteenth and twentieth centuries, the roles of the cook and chef had to make great strides to keep pace with advancements in sciences and technologies and to meet the growing demands of the emerging discipline.

One who had enormous influence on the profession early on was the great French chef Auguste Escoffier (author of *Le Guide Culinaire*, 1902). By the time he laid down his knife, chefs had fully emerged as artisans—artisans with a scientific precision. Recipes, along with the cooking techniques required to make them, became standardized and tested throughout the modern world. Even the kitchen was reorganized by Escoffier, to generate greater efficiencies and enable cooks and chefs to prepare outstanding food with precision and consistent quality. From the apprentice to the executive chef, the stations of the kitchen were established, along with well-defined roles and responsibilities. To this day, ACF's certification program requires candidates to reference the works of Escoffier as the foundation of modern cooking.

By the turn of the twentieth century, America had earned a reputation for fine food—though it still "borrowed" most of its celebrity chefs from European countries. Charles Ranhofer, who worked for Delmonico's in New York City from 1862 to1894, was perhaps the first French chef to make a name for himself in an American restaurant. When, in 1893, the Waldorf Hotel opened at the opposite end of Manhattan in direct competition to Delmonico's, the battle to attract customers and keep them coming back was underway.

Competition in the culinary and hospitality industry continued to intensify from that point forward, until the stock market crash in 1929 (ironically, the same year the ACF was formed). As for virtually all industries across the board, the years of the Great Depression had a devastating effect on the hospitality industry, and it wasn't until after World War II that American restaurants, hotels, and resorts began to prosper once again.

6

This once again opened opportunities for employment, but this time to a new class of American trained cooks and chefs. For the immigration of trained European chefs to America began to slow at the same time culinary schools in this country began opening their doors. In 1946, the Culinary Institute of America was one of the first to focus its educational programs on professional cooking at its New Haven, Connecticut, campus. Today there are more than 1,000 professional-track culinary educational programs in the United States, and hundreds more worldwide.

During the latter half of the twentieth century, hundreds of restaurant concepts were tested and dozens of chain restaurants and new hotels were launched. With each opening new career opportunities for the cook and chef presented themselves, and ultimately grew to encompass all economic strata and cross all cultural and geographic boundaries.

THE FUTURE OF THE CULINARY PROFESSION

Today's modern cooks and chefs must be flexible and adept in order to survive in this large and varied industry. They can no longer afford to train for, say, just grand hotels, or private clubs, or fancy restaurants; rather, they must have capabilities that apply to the larger industry, that incorporate all facets of food styles and service. It is by having multiple skills, varied experience, and a broad knowledge of food and drinks that a modern culinarian can help ensure his or her success.

The ACF's certification program was designed to accommodate these broad-based professional careers, which all share a similar profile of education, training, and execution. The types of foodservice and hospitality operations may be diverse, but the parameters that support them are all the same: good, healthy food; outstanding service; fair value; and a clean, safe environment in which to enjoy them. The modern professional cook and chef must study and train in all facets of quality foodservice to maximize their career potentials. Though cooking and baking remain the foundation upon which all professional chef careers are based, today's culinarians are expected to also know

7

about sanitation and food safety, nutritional cooking, food costs, supervision, and management.

Notably, those entering culinary administration, a new tract for foodservice professionals in the twenty-first century, must acquire business and financial management skills equal to or better than their cooking and baking knowledge, in order to supervise large and complex foodservice and hospitality operations. Though they will supervise chefs and the production and service of the food, their greater concerns often will be costs, expenses, and profits of the operation for which they are responsible. Together with the chefs and pastry chefs they supervise, they must function as a team, relying on each other's strengths, if they are to run large, popular, and profitable organizations.

It is through ACF certification that all culinary team players can be assured of having the skills and knowledge they need to do the jobs they are hired for. At all levels of the profession, in all facets of the foodservice industry, it takes the ACF framework of skills and knowledge, coupled with a continuous drive to learn and share that learning, that defines today's professional chef.

The Significance of ACF Certification

IN THE 30-PLUS YEARS SINCE ITS LAUNCH IN 1974, the ACF certification program has been tested, revised, and improved to meet the ever-growing demands and challenges of the foodservice industry. The program has been scrutinized by many national and international agencies to ascertain the integrity of its delivery mechanisms and the validity of its outcomes. Do the cooks and chefs certified by the ACF meet the claims of the program? Are they prepared, at the level they are certified, to meet the prerequisites of the positions they will ultimately fill? Do the foundational subjects of the program remain relevant in the modern industry? Are all the requirements stringent enough to certify only those qualified?

The answer continues to be a resounding yes.

BUILDING THE ACF CERTIFICATION LADDER

When Chefs Brown, Braun, and Metz formulated the first ACF certification guidelines, they were representing more than 50 years of ACF history. By that time, the ACF membership was well represented in major hotels, restaurants, and clubs around America. This gave the three chefs sufficient direction and guidance, which, coupled with their own experiences, helped them to devise the first formulas for certification.

In the intervening years, the ACF certification process has undergone much debate and review. Indeed, ongoing research, review, and debate are essential to ensure that the ACF certification program remains viable as the industry and the role chefs play in it continue to undergo change. For just as certification validates an individual's background and accomplishments, the world culinary market validates the integrity of ACF certification. This is important, because ACF-certified cooks and chefs are sought after by many American corporations, clubs, private restaurants, and schools. Some organizations even dictate that hiring decisions, promotions, and raises be contingent on obtaining and/or upgrading professional certification. As a result, those who wear ACF insignias have been embraced by the nation's restaurants, hotels, and clubs.

ACF's Certification Program has also been embraced by other countries around the world, an acknowledgment of its well-defined organization and consistent quality of delivery. Chefs in Canada, Mexico, and many Latin American countries have witnessed close-hand the ACF Certification Program and how it has helped to develop and promote professionalism in the industry. They seek to mirror the same pedagogy in their own chef certification programs. In Singapore, Egypt, and Korea, too, chefs have shown an interest in ACF's Certification Program, recognizing the value it brings to the professional life of those in the foodservice and hospitality industry. Like the ACF, these foreign chefs' associations are members of the World Association of Cooks Society (WACS), a global community of cooks and chefs.

It is through ACF's participation in WACS that its certification program has earned worldwide recognition. In particular, those WACS member organizations that do not have their own certification programs often look to the ACF's when developing or implementing one in their own countries. This cross-culture exchange is possible because although recipe ingredients, flavors, and presentation styles may vary among nations, cooking and baking practices around the world are based on the same fundamentals. Thus, it follows that the skills and knowledge required to be successful cooks and chefs also are similar globally.

CLIMBING THE RUNGS OF THE ACF LADDER

In the past, successful chefs started their apprenticeships at a much earlier age, and performed many more fundamental and parochial duties and tasks than their counterparts today. Some of the world's most famous chefs—for example Antoine Carême, who would one day be called, alternately, the King of Chefs and the Chef of Kings, and Auguste Escoffier, considered the father of modern cuisine—had humble if not dire beginnings. Carême worked day and night, under grueling circumstances, for a famous French baker named Bailly in a patisserie, an experience that honed both his skills and his character. Escoffier started his apprenticeship at the age of thirteen under his uncle, who swore he would not show the young Auguste any favoritism. For them, and thousands more like them, hard work, discipline, perseverance, and a propensity for learning proved to be the enduring tools of the trade, which both sharpened their personal skills and eventually led to their professional success.

Though aspiring culinarians today may not face the same hardships, they must deal with a much more complex industry, and as they begin their careers, they may feel lost in the maze of the demands imposed on them; they undoubtedly will feel daunted when comparing their status against the prestige of the executive chefs they will be reporting to and those they have heard and read about. They will need to be assured that their own goal of rising to the top is possible.

To that end, the ACF certification program is designed to follow the natural progression of the culinarian's career from cook to master chef; as such, it provides an ideal career ladder that foodservice professionals can climb in clearly defined increments. Each level is based on a specific amount of experience and knowledge, which continues to build as they climb to the top. Along the way, it offers both short- and long-term goals to inspire and motivate the aspirant culinarian.

Each step of the ACF certification ladder represents a turning point in a professional cook's or chef's career path. Each is an achievement, indicating that the student has proven his or her skills and knowledge in both the kitchen and the classroom, and therefore is properly trained and motivated to do the job they are asked to perform.

First Steps

Certified Culinarian (CC) and Pastry Culinarian (CPC) are the first levels of ACF certification. They acknowledge the culinarian who has made his or her commitment to the profession of cooking and baking. A Certified Culinarian has a minimum of three years' full-time experience in cooking and/or baking (for Pastry Culinarian). This person has demonstrated:

- Knowledge in cooking and baking fundamentals, sanitation, food safety, nutrition, nutritional cooking, supervision, and management.
- Solid cooking or baking skills, by performing well in a practical cooking/baking test under the scrutiny of experienced chefs and pastry chefs.

The designations Certified Culinarian and Pastry Culinarian are in and of themselves marks of great achievements and have signaled the beginning of many exciting careers. A Certified Culinarian/Pastry Culinarian is well prepared to succeed at this level and progress to the next.

After a culinarian has worked three or more years in a professional kitchen, he or she is ready to assume greater cooking and station responsibilities—although the size and complexity of the operation will determine the number and type of positions and how quickly promotions can be made. Young culinarians

12

should aim to gain as wide a variety of experiences as possible in their developing years to give themselves more options as they advance in their careers.

Stepping Up

Once a culinarian can prove that he or she can successfully manage multiple and complex tasks, and be responsible for their outcomes, they are typically put in a supervisory role, directing and advising lower-level culinarians such as preparation cooks and assistant line cooks in the performance of related tasks. This marks a major shift in a culinarian's career to supervisor and manager. The experiences gained at this juncture go a long way toward shaping his or her leadership qualities, and so will impact the direction of the culinarian's future.

At this critical level of their development, culinarians can seek to earn designation as a Certified Sous Chef (CSC) or Working Pastry Chef (CWPC). A CSC is someone who has demonstrated the ability to supervise other people in the performance of their duties while managing diverse and integrated procedures themselves. CWPCs have demonstrated the ability to manage multiple baking and pastry tasks; and though they may not supervise other pastry workers their own levels of responsibility for production and quality control become great assets. At this level, each person, in his or her field of expertise, has proven to be competent in a larger set of skills and knowledge and has crossed the line from worker to supervising manager successfully.

WHAT'S IN A NAME?
Culinary titles vary from operation to operation: someone may be called a line cook in one operation but a first cook in another. That is why the ACF certification verification process measures levels of responsibilities, not titles, through both written and practical tests.

Similarly, each of the succeeding ACF certification levels indicate achievements at increasingly difficult and complex positions. Personal Chef (PCC), Chef de Cuisine (CCC), Executive Chef (CEC), and Executive Pastry Chef (CEPC) certifications each designate individuals with specific training and experiences.

Whether they learned those skills and gained their knowledge through formal or on-the-job training is irrelevant, compared to their comprehension of the subject matter and their ability to apply what they know in practice.

Top Rung

The pinnacle to which all culinarians aspire is the highest level of ACF certification: Certified Master Chef (CMC) and Master Pastry Chef (CMPC), which are comparable to other prestigious master chef programs in Europe and Asia. Those designations say, incontrovertibly, that the person displaying either of these insignias has achieved the utmost in professional experience, has gained the highest level of skills and knowledge in all areas of professional foodservice, and has consistently demonstrated a high level of success in all areas of the kitchen. In short, Master Chefs and Master Pastry Chefs are truly masters of their craft.

RELATIVELY SPEAKING

Chefs can also specialize in various related cooking fields and thus earn "relative" ACF certifications. For example, culinarians entering the private chef industry, those who cook for families in their homes, can earn certification as personal chefs and personal executive chefs (for accumulated years of experience); educators can seek certification for secondary (high schools) and postsecondary experience. In all cases, ACF certification is based on the same foundations of knowledge, progressive skill development, and demonstration of proficiencies.

WHAT ACF CERTIFICATION MEANS TO THE MARKETPLACE

All those who employ, work with, and are served by ACF-certified individuals are beneficiaries of the ACF certification program.

Certification tells potential employers that applicant chefs and cooks have the knowledge and skill required for the positions for which they are applying. Certification provides professional cooks and chefs with concrete credentials that can differ-entiate their applications from dozens if not hundreds of others that cross potential employers' desks.

Certification offers assurance to consumers that the food they order will not only be delicious, but safe as well as pre-pared to highest quality standards possible. The latter is now more important than ever as concerns about food safety and healthy cooking (diet trends) continue to be on the rise in this country. ACF-certified cooks and chefs have made a commit-ment to the public to provide the best, safest food possible. Without certification, consumers can only hope for the best; with ACF-certified chefs, they are assured of getting it.

The ACF Validation Process: Meeting Measurable Objectives

THE PRIMARY PURPOSE OF A PROGRESSIVE CERTIFICATION PRO-
GRAM LIKE THE ACF's is to guide aspiring cooks and chefs
through the various stages of their professional development,
setting milestones for accomplishments and with an end goal in
sight. Certification is a voluntary process that can improve the
chances for personal success of those who choose to participate.
So, although it cannot be said that all successful cooks and chefs
are certified, it can be said that only those who are have met the
high standards established by the American Culinary
Federation. It is also important to point out what distinguishes
certification: it validates what culinary professionals have
accomplished, not what they hope to accomplish or say they
have accomplished. That is, certification is neither an award to
win nor a grade to earn; it is a mark of professionalism, one that
is achievable only through study, practice, and experience.

The ACF certification testing, reporting, and verification
processes have been designed to ensure that certification candi-

dates at all levels can successfully perform the duties and responsibilities of the positions for which they seek certification. Candidates must be able to:

- Document their learning and experiences
- Prove competency in food knowledge, sanitation, supervision, and nutrition
- Produce foods or baked goods commensurate with the skills demonstrated by paid professionals working at the same level

Only then are candidates certified and allowed to join the proud ranks of other certified cooks and chefs. If they cannot prove themselves, they will be denied certification until they can.

Certification, then, can be thought of as an insurance program: It ensures that specific levels of knowledge and skill have been dutifully learned and properly tested by a nationally recognized professional organization, and meet or exceed industry standards. Professional cooks and chefs who earn their American Culinary Federation certifications also are awarded the confidence of fellow culinarians, their employers, and their customers.

 ## HOW THE ACF CERTIFICATION PROGRAM WORKS

The only way to consistently judge the experiences and competencies of professionals is to establish a comprehensive set of guidelines, underlain by a solid methodology. Through a series of checks and balances, the ACF certification process can, to a high degree of accuracy, predict success for those who earn its designations. As noted, certified chefs have proven they have the skills and knowledge to fulfill the positions they hold now and in the future; the same cannot be said for noncertified cooks and chefs.

As the culinary profession expands to meet the needs of the growing foodservice and hospitality industry, its members are, of course, expected to raise the level of their culinary, supervisory, business, and management skills accordingly. The ACF Certification Program helps them do that, by mirroring in its processes the level of complexity and demands of the practice. Thus, the renewal certification processes ensure that each ACF-certified member is, essentially, on "top of his or her game."

By thoroughly examining all the attributes that comprise the roles and responsibilities of the professional cook and chef [e.g., their ability to cook, bake, teach (for educators), or supervise large complex foodservice operations], the ACF assures employers and the public alike that each certified cook or chef will continue to be successful and reliable.

BACKGROUND OF ACF DEVELOPMENT

A reputable certification program must be based on national industry standards. In the case of the ACF, that means that a cook who is certified in New York must have the same skills, knowledge, and experiences as cooks who are certified in San Francisco; likewise, cooks who are certified in rural America must also be qualified to compete for jobs in major urban centers. Again, a culinarian needs the same basic skills and knowledge to be successful wherever he or she works.

By 1974, when it launched its fully developed certification program, the ACF already had a reputation as a leader in collecting, analyzing, and chronicling culinary standards from all corners of the United States and other parts of the world. So thorough was the work of its earliest leaders that today's structure is based on a chapter system devised by the three chefs organizations that were its founding members in 1929: the Vatel Club, the Société Culinaire Philanthropique, and the Executive Chef de Cuisine of America, all three New York–based associations. The members of these organizations recognized from the start the importance both of unity and individuality. Therefore, rather than dissolve their organizations to form a composite, they joined as member organizations, giving birth to the chapter system.

The ACF now has more than 250 chapters nationwide, representing cooks and chefs in all 50 states. As noted in Chapter 1, it is also a participating member in the World Association of Cooks Society (WACS), a global cooking association composed of more than 70 country members, formed in 1928 and incorporated one year earlier than the ACF. Together, ACF and WACS form a far-reaching network of cooks, chefs, educators, administrators, and research chefs, who represent all facets of the industry worldwide, thus enabling widespread sharing of skills and knowledge.

It wasn't until 1962 that the ACF produced the first training manual for culinary apprentices. This was done under the leadership of then-president Willy Rossel, who at the time was executive chef of the Sheraton Hotel in Dallas, Texas. As contributors and reviewers he enlisted the help of over a dozen of the country's leading chefs. Called *The Apprentice Manual,* the publication became a model for authors and publishers of other textbooks and apprentice journals for years to come.

The ACF reaffirmed its commitment to professional training and formal education in 1974, when the certification program was launched, and again in 1986, when the ACF formed its Accrediting Commission to evaluate formal culinary art educational programs. Today the ACF Apprenticeship Committee, Certification Committee, and Accrediting Commission all function under the auspices of the American Culinary Federation Foundation, unified by a single mission: to educate and train culinarians.

To maintain the integrity of its mission, the ACF aggressively seeks and examines all the information available on trends; new technologies; international cuisine; and the growing demands placed on foodservice operations and its cooks, chefs, and managers. Its findings are integrated into its evolving educational programs.

In 1999, for example, the ACF hired an unbiased polling and survey company, Knapp and Associates International of Princeton, New Jersey, to investigate independently the current skills and competencies of American cooks and chefs coast to coast. More than 12,000 cooks and chefs at all levels participated, and critical information on jobs, duties, and responsibilities was meticulously researched and, ultimately, published.

What the ACF trustees found upon examining the results of the study and comparing them to published ACF standards were striking similarities. The ACF guidelines required only a few changes, which in due course were made.

The Knapp Study concluded that the process the ACF had developed to train and promote the culinary profession was accurate and consistent with current practices in American kitchens and bakeshops.

SETTING MEASURABLE OBJECTIVES

A culinarian's professional goals are achieved by developing proficiencies in a progressive sequence of tasks and knowledge-based competencies, beginning with basic food preparation and, after many years of study and experience, advancing to classical, international, and modern cuisines. As one of their competencies, for example, novice culinarians must be able to identify and prepare a variety of vegetables, utilizing various cooking techniques, (prepare for service entails more than cooking techniques: let's state instead "cooking and presentation techniques") according to industry standards. Master chefs, at the other end of the certification spectrum, must be able to do the same but utilizing international and classical cooking techniques, flavors, and presentations. The difference of course is the level of expertise with which each is expected to demonstrate competency. The objective may be the same, to identify and prepare vegetables, but the measure of expertise is how many types of vegetables, cooking procedures, and different cuisine styles the cook can use in selecting and preparing them.

The point is, professional culinary skills have thousands of measurable competencies by which expertise is judged and positions are identified. Cooks are expected to demonstrate certain competencies, sous chefs others, and pastry chefs others still. The mastery of those competencies are, then, the objectives that each culinarian must achieve as they learn to perform the jobs at each level of certification. As they meet those objectives, culinarians compile the basis for their ACF certifications.

MEASURING PERFORMANCE OBJECTIVES

To measure competency in job performance objectives, the ACF employs a three-tiered system:

1. Validate success on the job (work history)
2. Validate skills through practical cooking and baking tests
3. Test knowledge

Each tier is designed to determine proficiency from a different perspective, ultimately to result in a complete picture of the level of professional cooking and/or baking skills and knowledge an individual has achieved.

Validating Success on the Job

Each level of ACF certification has specific requirements related to a candidate's personal work history. It is generally based on the type of operation in which a person works, his or her position there, and how long he or she was employed by that particular operation. Collectively, a series of operations and jobs makes up the typical certification candidacy.

A specific requirement is also assigned for each certification level, based on the number of years a person has already worked in the position for which he or she is applying. For the novice culinarian, that means any professional cooking job, for that is the lowest rung on the career ladder; but for other certifications, the requirement is highly specific. For example, a person applying for certification as a sous chef must have been a sous chef (using the ACF definition) for at least two years, in addition to three years in any culinary position. An executive chef candidate must have already held positions as executive chef, or head chef, for a minimum of five years, and up to seven years, depending on how may different employers that person has served. In addition to the required experience, executive chef candidates must be able to document a minimum of three more years in progressive cooking positions, leading to the one they currently hold as executive chef.

These experiential requirements are necessary not only to prove that each candidate has the requisite cooking and or baking skills, but that those skills have been tested through practical job experience in the foodservice industry. A person can learn cooking skills in hundreds if not thousands of different places, but before the ACF will grant certification, the candidate must be able to prove that he or she can successfully hold professional cooking and baking jobs.

Naturally, the number of experiential years required to climb each rung on the certification ladder is different. Specific matrices are based on the degree of difficulty and level of responsibilities in the positions held. A certified culinarian requires only three years of full-time experience in any professional cooking and/or baking position (for Certified Pastry Culinarian); a sous chef requires a minimum of five years of experience, and an executive chef requires documentation of a minimum of seven years of progressively professional culinary experience. In all cases, experience must be documented and verifiable, as it becomes the building blocks upon which certification is based.

Validating Skills Proficiency

For the past 20 to 30 years, the culinary/hospitality industry has expanded faster and experienced greater change than most other service industries, a trend that shows no sign of slowing in the twenty-first century. One consequence of this growth was that it became more difficult to differentiate the educated, skilled, and dedicated culinary professionals from the myriad others who were not equally qualified. Another consequence was the generation of more jobs for trained cooks and chefs than there were seasoned culinarians to fill them. That is not to say that there was a shortage of *applications* for every job posted, but a shortage of qualified candidates.

At the same time, awareness was growing in the professional culinary community and the public at large of the dangers connected both with unsafe food practices and unhealthy eating habits. Unsafe food practices, resulting in outbreaks of mad cow disease, *E. coli,* the Norwalk virus, hepatitis A, and others became front-page news around the world. Unhealthy eating habits caused an outbreak of trendy diets, such as Atkins, low-fat, low-sodium, and, most recently, low-carb. The foodservice industry has had to respond to both these concerns.

Finally, prices for food ingredients and the cost of labor escalated exponentially over the last several years; coupled with increased competition, virtually every operation has been forced to streamline and control costs. In sum, the need for versatile and experienced professional cooks and chefs has never been greater.

For its part, the ACF was called upon to stay abreast of these changes and to further ensure proficiency in the craft. To answer the call, the Certification Committee took action and, after many months of input, discovery, and debate, in January 2003, added practical cooking and baking exams to its certification program as another level of skill verification. They created an observable and measurable process by which to verify each candidate's cooking and/or baking abilities, in addition to their other skills and knowledge.

Now all cooks and chefs who seek ACF certification must prove proficiency through a demonstration of their cooking and/or baking skills at the level of the certification they seek. Here are three ways they can do that:

- Pass an official ACF practical exam through one of its sponsoring chapters, accredited schools, or during an ACF conference or convention.
- Earn a silver or gold medal in any ACF-sanctioned Category F/1: Hot Food Professional cooking competition, for cooking candidates, or F/5: Pastry Mystery Basket competition, for pastry candidates, according to ACF competition guidelines. These are four-hour competitions that incorporate a variety of preparation and presentation techniques. A silver medal or better indicates a high level of proficiency.
- Earn a silver or gold medal in any WACS-sanctioned hot-food competition, either as an individual or as a member of a team of chefs.

24

Other practical skill-testing methodologies can be used to fulfill the ACF skill proficiency requirement (which constitutes a request for waiver of the skill proficiency requirement), but they must be delivered in a disciplined environment, incorporate a sufficient amount of diverse skill assessments and measurable competencies, and be scrutinized and graded by qualified, certified professionals.

Sanctioned examiners must be proven professionals who have undertaken additional training in the objective evaluation of culinary proficiency based on national and international standards. Requests for a waiver of the skill proficiency requirement must be accompanied by a full description of the test, the credentials or authority of the person or company delivering the test, and an official, verifiable document or certificate of successful completion. In short, to satisfy the certification requirement, test results must demonstrate the same rigor, discipline, and integrity as the ACF testing program.

In all cases, the intent is to measure proficiency of each candidate, at a specific level, under the supervision of trained and experienced examiners and/or competition judges.

Testing Knowledge

The ACF Certification Program expects, and measures, specific levels of education for each level of certification. All culinarians must have a basic foundation of knowledge, and as they progress up the certification ladder, they must obtain and demonstrate higher levels of cognitive proficiencies in a greater variety of subjects. Cognitive learning can be measured by many different tools, and the ACF requires multiple levels of proof to ensure a fair and equitable evaluation of a person's level of achievement.

A grounding of knowledge in specific subjects and the commitment to continuing education are the foundations of all ACF certification levels. Formal education, corporate training, apprenticeship training, self-study programs, Internet, and correspondence courses give even hard-working professionals many opportunities for continuing their education and meeting the requirements of ACF certification.

To become successful at increasingly more difficult and

complex jobs, such as sous chef and executive chef, professionals must be very knowledgeable in three critical areas: sanitation, nutrition, and supervision. Therefore, these three topics are mandatory courses for ACF certification. That is, all candidates for certification must provide proof of practical learning in these three areas. Thirty hours of classroom learning or its equivalent is required for each subject, plus a five-year renewal obligation. That means each candidate must take an additional eight hours of instruction in the same areas every five years. In this way, the ACF helps ensure that all ACF-certified chefs have current knowledge in the critical areas of food safety, health, and management.

The courses must be taken under the auspices of an accredited school or one of many ACF-approved institutional programs, to assure that specific competencies will be delivered in a formal, organized, and integral process, and led by a qualified instructor. Proof of obtaining or enhancing knowledge can be provided in the form of school transcripts, official certificates, or letters of confirmation.

Culinary, sanitation, nutrition, management, and business knowledge for each candidate is measured by a comprehensive written exam. Each test is composed of a variety of questions derived from a database of more than 5,000 questions categorized into 12 different subject matters. Not all subjects are used in all categories of certifications, but where they are used, their weight of importance (whether they make up 5, 10, 15, or 20 percent of the total test matrix) is determined by the level of responsibilities and expertise the position carries, as follows:

MAKING IT MANDATORY
You'll learn more about this mandatory coursework in Chapter 4, "A Foundation in Learning."

1. Basic cooking
2. Basic baking
3. Sanitation and safety
4. Nutrition/nutritional cooking
5. Supervision and management
6. Advanced cooking (including classical cooking)

7. Advanced baking
8. Human resources management [Certified Culinary Administrator (CCA) certification only]
9. Strategic management (CCA only)
10. Operational management (CCA only)
11. Education development [Certified Secondary Culinary Educators (CSCE) and Culinary Educators (CCE) only]
12. Education psychology (CSCE and CCE only)

Written tests must be taken for each initial grant of ACF certification and when upgrading a certification level. To maintain a certification level over its five-year renewal period, each person must document a certain number of hours of continuing education in culinary, culinary management, or business-related subjects.

CONCLUSION

Culinary technologies and trends continue to develop every day, and the studies regarding foodservice become more in-depth (particularly in the areas of sanitation and nutrition). To keep one's skills honed requires continuous research, discussion, and study. Thus, the importance of having a solid foundation in culinary knowledge, one that grows with each level of certification, cannot be overstated. To truly master this craft, practitioners must be adept in all of its aspects. Cooks and chefs must know about foods, what they are, where they come from, what benefits they contain, and the proper techniques for preparing them, as handed through generations of culinary development. It is not surprising that this requires a lifetime of learning.

CHAPTER 4

Laying a Foundation in Learning

WHETHER SERVING IN HUMBLE POSITIONS AS CRAFTSPEOPLE AND DOMESTICS (private residence cooks) or holding prestigious positions in clubs, hotels, and other complex foodservice operations, cooks and chefs throughout the centuries have dedicated their lives to the study and improvement of culinary arts. Those who became renowned devoted their professional lives to the study and improvement of culinary art, and by doing so made the profession better for all culinarians. For example, Chef Guillaume Tirel (c. 1310–1395), the lead cook in the court of King Philippe VI of France in the middle of the fourteenth century and author of the first cookbook on French cuisine, *Le Viandier*, was one of the first to recognize the importance of study and practice to his craft. François-Pierre de la Varenne, chef under the Marquis d'Uxelles, Louis Chalon du Blé, was another devoted student of culinary arts. He became a great innovator of seventeenth-century French cuisine and wrote many culinary books to share what he knew. And Antoine Carême (1784–1833), whom we

29

spoke of in Chapter 2 (the King of Chefs and the Chef of Kings), is known to have studied his culinary texts by candlelight after working 12 to 14 hours per day.

As the foodservice profession evolves, so too must its technicians, practitioners, and educators if they are to maintain their competitive edge and help their employers do the same.

CLASSICAL CUISINES SET THE STANDARD

It is not uncommon to hear the claim that there is nothing new in cooking, that there are only new interpretations and reinventions of what has been already been done. To some degree this is understandable, for modern culinary art in the West is founded on the classical cooking techniques of eighteenth- and nineteenth-century Europe. There, time-tested cooking, baking, and food presentation procedures were standardized after hundreds of years of evolution by the aforementioned French chefs, Antoine Carême, Auguste Escoffier, and a handful of others. Cuisines of the East, including Indian, Asian, and Middle Eastern, also have classical foundations, specific to their cultures and cuisines, and followed by modern chefs in today's cooking techniques, recipes, and presentations.

During these centuries, in the great kitchens around the world, the chefs who led them standardized and applied cooking procedures, which eventually became regarded as basic techniques from which all future recipes should be based. *Leading sauces* (sometimes referred to as *mother sauces*), proper cooking techniques, cuts of meat and vegetables, and thousands of recipes with specific cooking treatments and garnishes were all standardized. As a result, cooks and chefs today from around the world can teach and learn from each other by referring to the same set of standardized recipes and procedures. For example, when a French chef in Paris refers to the sauce espagnole (brown mother sauce) or hollandaise, he or she is talking about the same sauce as chefs in London, Moscow, Frankfurt, New York, and Mexico City. Likewise, cooking techniques such as stock making, braising, sautéing, and stir-frying are so well defined that cooks and chefs around the world know how to perform them properly.

But the presence of standards *does not* mean the absence of innovation. So the claim that there are no new recipes is false. In fact, new recipes are developed every day, and new and different presentations arise from time to time. That said, frying is still frying, poaching is still poaching, and baking is still baking. The technologies to perform them might change, but the science that makes them work does not.

PRESENTING THE CLASSICS FOR CERTIFICATION

ACF certification requires knowledge and experience of the cooking techniques and standardized sauces and procedures now considered "classical." In both its written and practical tests, classical cooking theory, recipes, and procedures are among the measurable objectives in which each candidate must demonstrate proficiency. Although neither test concentrates on classical foundations, both are considered paramount to the success of each ACF-certified cook and chef. And though students are expected to demonstrate creativity and be capable of employing modern cooking techniques and presentations in the practical cooking and baking tests, any reference made to classical items must follow exactly the procedures so defined.

The reference the test examiners use to verify classical authenticity is Auguste Escoffier's *Le Guide Culinaire* (commonly known in English as the *Escoffier Cookbook*). No other resource is considered authentic, and no modern interpretations of the classics are permitted. If, say, the test asks the candidate to define or make a velouté sauce (one of the five leading sauces), the standard used to measure success comes from Escoffier. If the operation a particular cook or chef works in adulterates a classical recipe by adding or deleting ingredients/procedures to or from

BY THE BOOK

Certification candidates are always advised to reference the *Escoffier Cookbook* before taking either test, to ensure they know the proper information and how to demonstrate it.

31

sauces and "named" dishes, those recipes and procedures will not be accepted as substitutes for the classic versions in ACF testing.

The leading sauces and the components needed to make them provide a good sample of the items for which a candidate may be expected to follow classical procedures:

- *Roux*: one part flour and one part clarified butter or neutral oil cooked slowly over a low heat source to produce three variations, determined by the length of cooking: white, blond, and brown roux
- *Velouté*: white veal or chicken stock thickened by a blond (pale) roux (veal meat optional)
- *Béchamel*: milk thickened by a white roux, seasoned lightly with nutmeg and thyme
- *Hollandaise*: an emulsified egg and butter sauce, which begins with a reduction of vinegar, white pepper, and salt
- *Espagnole*: browned beef/veal stock thickened by a brown roux, with the addition of tomatoes, carrots, celery, and onions (mirepoix) for the last part of the cooking process
- *Tomato*: butter or olive oil, flour, salt pork, carrots, onions, and thyme cooked together until light brown and used to thicken tomatoes, tomato puree, and white stock; seasoned with garlic
- *Mirepoix*: finely diced carrots, onions, and celery, sautéed in pork fat with thyme and bay leaf
- *Matignon*: finely minced carrots, onions, and celery with lean ham, thyme, and bay leaf, which is then cooked lightly in butter

Some of the practical cooking tests ask the candidates to write a menu from a basket of ingredients, and then to prepare the menu of items following proper cooking and plating procedures. The instructions do not require that classical recipes be used, but if they are, they must be produced using *Escoffier's Cookbook* as the main reference. For example, cooking terms such as *fricassee, braise, poach, stew,* and *sauté* are defined by Escoffier as specific cooking procedures utilizing certain types of ingredients, procedures, and pans. Those procedures must be followed exactly as Escoffier described them.

In their menus, candidates may name dishes (this is not required) from Escoffier's and other leading international classical chefs, dishes such as Homard à la Américaine (Lobster American style) or Suprêmes de Volaille aux Champignons (boneless chicken breasts sautéed and served with mushrooms). Again, should they choose to do this, *Escoffier's Cookbook* is the model against which the ACF compares the results.

CROSS-TRAINING IN CULINARY FUNDAMENTALS

The ACF requires all professional culinarians, no matter what level or position they hold, to have a good understanding of all aspects of culinary arts. That is to say, cooks must know cooking, but they also must understand the basics of baking and *garde-manger* (pantry/cold foods); conversely, bakers must know baking procedures, but they should also be familiar with cooking terms and applications.

The reason, according to the ACF, is threefold:

1. By cross-training all the employees in a culinary operation, consistency is ensured, for no matter how busy the operation or a single department becomes, all staff will be capable of helping out where needed.
2. Cross-trained professional culinarians have more options when it comes to job opportunities and are often promoted more quickly thanks to their proficiency in multiple skills.
3. Those aspiring to executive chef and all other supervising chef levels need to have knowledge of everything they supervise; they are not required to be the expert in everything, but knowledgeable enough to enable them to guide others in the performance of their work.

The ACF Top 40-Plus

The ACF has classified 40-plus culinary subjects into either basic or advanced cooking and baking categories. These topics represent the fundamental information all culinarians should strive to learn to become successful in the modern industry. Certified culinarians should be learned in the two basic categories of subjects, with their level of knowledge progressing into the advanced cooking and baking categories as they continue to develop their professional portfolios.

1. BASIC COOKING:
   a. Cooking principles and processing terminology
   b. Kitchen equipment
   c. Food items and ingredients
   d. Seasonings, flavorings, spices, and herbs
   e. Stocks and thickening agents
   f. Soups and sauces
   g. Breakfast and egg cookery
   h. Beef, veal, pork, and lamb cuts, and classifications
   i. Meat cookery
   j. Poultry and game classifications and cooking
   k. Fish and shellfish classifications and cooking
   l. Vegetables, pasta, potatoes, and rice classifications and cooking
   m. Salads and salad dressings
   n. Food purchasing
   o. Storeroom, inventory, and cost control procedures

2. BASIC BAKING:
   a. Bakery ingredients and equipment
   b. Yeast products and quick breads
   c. Pies and simple pastries
   d. Cakes and cookies
   e. Custards and fillings
   f. Frozen desserts
   g. Dessert sauces
   h. Baking formulas, yields, and costing

3. ADVANCED COOKING:
   a. Classical cuisine
   b. Garde-manger and charcuterie (smoked, cured, and dried meat products)
   c. International cuisine
   d. Hot-line prepared desserts

    e. American cuisine
    f. Menu planning

4. ADVANCED BAKING AND PASTRY:
    a. Classical desserts
    b. Candies
    c. Specialty cakes (e.g., wedding, anniversary cakes)
    d. Fancy cakes and tortes
    e. Fancy pastries
    f. Fancy cookies, petits fours sec and glacé (glazed)
    g. International desserts

Each of these subject areas is important to professional food-service, hence the importance of the mastery of them to the professional chef. As stated repeatedly, the higher up the career ladder a culinarian climbs, the more expertise he or she is required to have in these specific areas.

The Big Three: Mandatory Courses in Sanitation, Nutrition, and Management

Recall that in the previous chapter we discussed briefly the courses that the ACF has established as mandatory for every certification candidate, no matter which area of foodservice he or she works. In addition to the courses listed above, these are the subjects considered as critical to the education of all cooks and chefs. The ACF regards these courses as critical for the dramatic impact they have on quality food production and service.

For all cooking levels of certification (Culinarian through Master Chef) the mandatory courses include:

- Sanitation and Safety
- Nutrition/Nutritional Cooking
- Supervision/Management

All candidates for certification must have had a minimum of 30 hours of instruction in each of these courses within five years of their application. For college students, this equates to a minimum of two semester credits in each subject.

As mentioned in Chapter 3, there are several ways of earning credits for ACF mandatory courses and continuing education requirements. In addition to college, candidates may take this coursework at:

- All schools and institutions accredited by a state or regional accrediting agency
- Official ACF apprenticeship programs employing "certified teachers" in each subject area and meeting or exceeding ACF standards

FOR MORE INFORMATION
Go to the ACF Web site, www.acfchefs.org, and click on Professional Development and Certification.

- Local ACF chapters offering courses that follow ACF guidelines and syllabi, use approved texts, and are taught by qualified teachers in each area of concentration
- ACF Approved Internet programs and correspondence programs
- National professional organizations and training companies offering ongoing courses, such as the National Restaurant Association's (NRA) ServSafe (Sanitation and Safety) program, and the American Hotel, Motel, and Lodging Association's (AHM&LA) management programs; or individual courses that follow ACF or other national standards and guidelines

Tracking Changes in the Big Three

These courses are so critically important to successful food-service that the ACF requires continuing study in each subject every five years, with eight being the minimum number of hours for each. The purpose of these "refresher courses" for culinarians is not to review what they have already learned, but to discover and become familiar with what is new and different in each of these subject areas.

Why is this five-year rule necessary? For a number of reasons. First, sanitation and safety rules, laws, and regulations change on average every 1.5 years, as new evidence about bacteriology and the protection of food continues to be collected, analyzed, and disseminated by health and safety officials. Also,

THE ACF'S FIVE-YEAR RULE

ACF certifications are granted to professional cooks and chefs for one five-year period, after which they must be renewed or advanced in order to maintain the use of the coveted insignias. This five-year rule applies both to certifications and mandatory course refreshers. The ACF's five-year refresher requirement in the three mandatory subject areas parallels the certification renewal time period for cooks and chefs. (Note: Some ACF certification advocates argue that five years is too long between updating coursework in these critical areas. They recommend study in sanitation, nutrition, and management be done on a more regular or continuous basis.)

new health hazards are identified, new studies prove new or disprove old theories, and new information about food and safe working conditions continues to emerge. Thus, what a person learned about these issues five years ago no longer accurately reflects the concerns and problems facing the modern cook and chef.

Nutritional information likewise continues to change as more evidence about food and its relationship to health is collected, studied, and analyzed. The process is ongoing: Investigative studies of this kind can take dozens of years to complete and involve hundreds if not thousands of participants. Then, the different factions affected by the studies (e.g., American Dietary Association, American Medical Association, the USDA, and food manufacturers) debate the results until more evidence can support (or disprove) their individual claims. For example, recent changes in nutritional knowledge have to do with the discovery of disease-fighting agents in foods known as phytochemicals and flavonoids. Before these discoveries, carbohydrates, proteins, fats, vitamins, and minerals were considered the major nutrients; now the list is longer. There is also new evidence on the importance of folate and selenium for fighting diseases, as well as the effects of other vitamins and minerals on human health.

And, as mentioned earlier, information about the effects of diet on health also continues to be examined. Fad diets—

low-carb, cholesterol-lowering, and salt-free, to name just a few—spark scientific and consumer attention on a regular basis. Nutritional claims are made and challenged almost on a daily basis. Thus, continuing study of the tenets of nutrition and the application of nutritional knowledge to cooking and baking is paramount to the delivery of healthy foods to people around the world.

In contrast to sanitation and nutrition, supervision and management theories do not change as dramatically or quickly; nevertheless, new perspectives are revealed regularly—topics such as motivating and team building are put forth, discussed, applied to work situations, then measured against company successes or failures. Managers, supervisors, and, therefore, chefs, must be able to measure their own supervisory effectiveness in light of new developments as they affect the production of quality food products and service. Adding to the challenge in this subject area is the growing dependence in this country on minority workers to fill vacant and new culinary positions. The changing face of the workforce also causes old theories of motivation and teamwork to be challenged, enhanced, and in some cases abandoned in light of new knowledge and corporate experiences. Cooks and chefs who expect to remain successful simply cannot afford to lead by following outdated rules, or they will lose their effectiveness until they themselves become liabilities to their employers.

Additional Mandatory Coursework for Educators

In addition to the mandatory courses all culinarians must take, culinary educators seeking ACF certification have to demonstrate proficiency in four other mandatory subject areas (which the ACF refers to as "educational development subjects") to reflect the fact that though they may teach cooking and baking, their primary "product" is the student. Thus, they have to be highly competent and current in human dynamics, educational theories, and other human psychometrics; and they too must improve, enhance, and continue to augment their understanding of the teaching and learning processes if they are to remain effective in the modern classroom.

ACF MANDATORY COURSE CURRICULA

Here are the specific areas of study in each of the three mandatory subject areas in which a culinarian must prove proficiency, both in understanding and application:

1. SANITATION AND SAFETY
   a. Foodborne illness
   b. Microbial contaminants
   c. Food allergies and intolerances
   d. Personal hygiene
   e. Safe flow of food through the operation
   f. Cleaning and sanitizing equipment and facilities
   g. Pest management
   h. Hazard Analysis Critical Control Point (HACCP) food safety program
   i. First aid
   j. Fire prevention
   k. Work hazard protection

2. NUTRITION/NUTRITIONAL COOKING
   a. Basic nutrition concepts: nutrition, kilocalories, nutrients
   b. Dietary reference intakes (DRI) for main nutrients
   c. Food guides, labels, and the USDA Food Guide Pyramid
   d. Functions of nutrients: carbohydrates, proteins, fats, vitamins, minerals, water
   e. Functions and availability of other disease-fighting nutrients: phytochemicals and flavonoids
   f. Healthy menu selections
   g. Recipes for better nutrition
   h. Weight management
   i. Nutrition and the human life cycle
   j. Health and nutrition

3. SUPERVISION AND MANAGEMENT
   a. Supervisory roles and responsibilities
   b. Management theories and practice
   c. Effective communication
   d. Motivational theory
   e. Leadership roles

f. Decision making and problem solving
g. Empowerment
h. Total Quality Management (TQM)
i. Team building
j. Quality work cultures
k. Diversity management
l. Americans with Disabilities Act (ADA)
m. Equal Employment Opportunities/Affirmative Action (EEO/AA)
n. Sexual harassment and discrimination
o. Drug and alcohol abuse
p. Ergonomics in the workplace

It should be clear by looking at these lists why the ACF considers continuous study in these areas an imperative for certification: Cooks and chefs cannot produce and deliver good, safe, healthy foods without a thorough knowledge of the three critical subjects affecting foodservice.

The ACF's four educational development subjects are:

- Curriculum Planning and Development (e.g., behavioral objectives, syllabi, lesson plans, etc.)
- Evaluation and Testing (e.g., practical, written, and oral testing)
- Teaching Methodology (e.g., kitchen laboratory, lecture, and nontraditional methods)
- Educational Psychology (e.g., learning styles and student motivation)

Cooks and chefs applying for culinary educator certification, at minimum, must have a bachelor's degree, or its equivalent, to qualify for either the secondary or postsecondary levels. And the requirement for education development coursework for secondary and postsecondary ACF Certified Educators is a minimum of 120 contact hours with concentrations in the four areas specified above.

Many colleges and state universities have teacher education programs offering a wide array of college courses that contain this fundamental curriculum content. Often, educational institutions design their own in-service teaching programs as a means of providing this coursework to their own faculty and staff.

PROGRESSIVE LEARNING

In addition to acquiring the foundations of culinary knowledge, which are necessary for all culinarians, progressive learning and advanced knowledge in culinary production and service throughout the world also are expected of all professional cooks and chefs.

Progressive learning can occur in myriad subjects affecting professional foodservice. The following are just a few suggestions to consider as you begin, or continue, your own professional development:

- *Classical cuisine.* The more thoroughly culinarians understand the achievements made in culinary arts over the last two centuries, the more effective they can be in today's kitchen.
- *International cuisine.* Simply put, it is incumbent upon professional cooks and chefs to learn about the different foods, drinks, recipes, and cooking and presentation styles of the world.
- *American/national cuisine.* No matter how well educated a culinarian becomes, there is always more to be learned about one's own food heritage and culture.
- *Advanced culinary.* In both cooking and baking, there are always higher pinnacles of culinary success and expertise to which a person can aspire.
- *Supervision and management.* With increased supervisory responsibilities comes a greater need to understand the concepts of motivation, teamwork, and workplace cultures.
- *Business/financial management.* The higher up the culinary career ladder a person climbs, the more he or she must pay

41

attention to the *business* of foodservice. It is critical for these "executives" to become just as proficient in running a business as they are in preparing fine foods and desserts.

In addition to the subjects listed here, there are a host of others that professional culinarians might be interested in exploring in greater detail, depending on their area of culinary expertise. These might include any or all of the following:

- Computer skills: hardware, software, and Internet proficiencies
- Business writing: business plans, communiqués, procedural manuals, and so on
- Food presentation/styling: designing and plating for individual servings and buffets
- Marketing: competitive strategies; research and development of customer base
- Public relations: building a presence within a community and developing a positive media relationship

CONTINUING EDUCATION

Whether certified culinarians choose to progress up the professional ladder or remain at a particular level, through a continuation of their education, they must stay current with the new techniques and ideas that continue to reshape the foodservice industry.

A culinarian can earn continuing education credits in a number of different ways to satisfy ACF requirements. Here are a few examples of ACF-preapproved continuing education resources for culinarians:

- All regional or state-accredited colleges, schools, and universities (many community college programs cater specifically to the professional, part-time student)
- All ACF nationally sponsored conferences, conventions, and workshops
- Participating ACF chapter educational programs

- National conventions of other leading professional organizations, including the National Restaurant Association; Retailer's Bakery Association; International Hotel, Motel, and Restaurant Association; International Foodservice Executives Association
- Industry-sponsored trade shows and exhibitions, for example: SYSCO, U.S Foodservice, and UBF (Unilever Best Foods) Solutions
- Programs offered by nationally recognized management and supervision management consulting companies, such as Dun & Bradstreet, Dale Carnegie, and Skill Path
- Corporate/military training programs
- ACF/WACS-sanctioned culinary competitions (must win bronze medal or higher to qualify for continuing education credit)
- ACF partner educational organizations, which include the American Hotel, Motel, and Lodging Association; American Academy of Independent Studies; chefcertification.com; and Steritech, Inc.
- Other formal education programs approved by the ACF education office

FOR MORE INFORMATION
Go to the ACF Web site, www.acfchefs.org, and click on Professional Development and Certification.

Whenever given the opportunity to take a class or participate in a workshop related to culinary production and service, culinarians are advised to do so, and to keep an official record of that participation (see Chapter 6 for more on this).

CONCLUSION

As we've said many times, a foundation in learning is the basis of ACF certification, and continuing education its strength. Professional cooks and chefs never tire of learning, for there is always something new to discover, share, cook, and taste. In the next chapter, you'll read how to incorporate ACF educational requirements as part of plotting your career path.

CHAPTER

5

Planning a Career Path in Foodservice

A CAREER IN THE FOODSERVICE INDUSTRY IS, fundamentally, a craft, and should be approached as such. In the beginning, you, as a young culinarian will proceed as any apprentice craftsperson, by starting on the bottom rung of the ladder—in this case, by focusing primarily on cooking and line-level management. As you advance, you will quickly become aware how much the industry has grown over the years, and continues to do so; you may even feel somewhat overwhelmed at the wide diversity of opportunities open to you, and in how many venues. You'll also quickly come to realize that to take advantage of one or more of these opportunities, you will need further education, in some cases, even a master's degree or doctorate.

With that in mind, you, the aspiring cook or chef, are well advised to strategically plot your career, specifically choreographing the moves you will make to accomplish your goals. In the course of this process, if you are wise, you will include certification as one of your goals, at least to the Executive Chef if

45

not the Culinary Administrator level. That decision will make it easier to continue plotting your moves, as you can follow the ladder developed by the American Culinary Federation. If followed from bottom to top, climbing the ACF ladder will take about 18 years, though some will advance quicker and skip either the Certified Sous Chef (CSC) or Certified Chef de Cuisine (CCC) "rungs." At a minimum, you should strive for the Certified Culinarian (CC), CSC, or CCC and Certified Executive Chef (CEC) designations, probably finishing with Certified Culinary Administrator (CCA).

CLASSIFYING CERTIFICATION

Chapter 7 details the 14 levels of ACF certification and the requirements for achievement in each.

From there it is possible to move to the level of Certified Master Chef (CMC) if you are so inclined, but this level requires much more than a simple progression through the levels and is not for every chef due to the required competencies that must be demonstrated. Hence, it must be a specifically designated goal in the career plan.

But goal setting is a dynamic process—a goal you set as a young cook of 18 will no doubt be revised at least once or twice. But, typically, the revised goal will be similar or associated with the original goal, therefore requiring only some minor redirection to the new goal, causing little interruption in education and loss of time.

CONSIDERING THE POSSIBILITIES

To lay a path that goes in the right direction to meet a defined goal requires seeking out reliable sources of information and advice from mentors. One of the most valuable features of the ACF is the ability to place yourself into venues that will allow you direct access to many different levels of professionals in varied fields of the food industry. Most of these people will make fantastic mentors and will be able to help you develop your career plan. You would also be advised to research as much as possible through the Internet and the many professional organizations to find other sources of career guidance. It also requires some soul-searching. You'll want to answer the following questions:

- *What type of life do you want to lead?* How important is family to you, and the time you spend with them? Many (not all) careers in foodservice will mean many nights, weekends, and holidays spent away from home. So any decision you make should involve your spouse or significant other and your family; you'll need the support from everyone close to you. The unfortunate fact is that there is a very high divorce rate among chefs, so before you get started, make sure your family understands your intentions as well as the demands of your job.
- *What type of work environment suits you best?* Do you thrive on stress? Are you a perfectionist? Do you like to work with a small or large group of people? Do you need a great deal of variety in your daily routine? Can you, literally, stand the heat in the kitchen? Are you driven by a frenzy of loud noises and action, or do you prefer a more quiet, corporate environment? The message is, conduct an *honest* self-appraisal and come to terms with what motivates you and what turns you off. Only then try to determine where in the foodservice industry you will fit in comfortably.
- *What type of people do you want to interact with on a daily basis?* Are they highly educated professionals, or do you enjoy a more "blue-collar" community, or perhaps a bit of both? And be aware that your perception of what is suitable may change with age.
- *Where do you want to live?* Keep in mind that demographics will dictate to some degree the style of food or type of business you want—where you prefer to live may not support a market for that particular business. For instance, a German-style restaurant in Fort Lauderdale, Florida, probably wouldn't be successful due to the demographics, weather, and the absence of widespread cultural understanding and desire for that cuisine. So if your dream is to open a German restaurant in a Florida beach town, clearly you will need to make some adjustments to your plan.

The important point here to remember is to stop at key points along your career path to reevaluate where you are going and how you will get there, gaining as much knowledge as possible in support of your career objective.

STAYING THE COURSE

You've no doubt heard the adage, "If it sounds too good to be true, it probably is." How this applies to your career path in the foodservice industry is that you may find yourself with the opportunity to reach a goal much more quickly than you expected. There is a very real danger in this profession of advancing too quickly, before you are ready. For example, say it's your first sous chef job, which you have been holding for two years. The executive chef leaves unexpectedly and, because management knows and trusts you, they offer you the position. Don't automatically say yes; instead, consider carefully: How will you continue to learn and grow while under the burden of a stressful challenge, which may be, in some respects, beyond your training or experience? More often than not in such a situation, the young chef becomes trapped; he or she is "too busy" to continue on the educational track or career path. Ultimately, this can be very detrimental to one's ultimate career goal and personal growth.

The prudent thing to do here is to discuss with management your concerns about your continued growth. Will they support you through tuition reimbursement, time off for continuing education, and encouragement for other endeavors you have set for yourself? These, of course, would include all things related to accomplishing certification and the training you need. Might they be willing to add staff to support your efforts—perhaps by employing an extra sous chef so that you are a bit freer to concentrate on becoming more knowledgeable through career development—and, thus, a better chef for the company? In sum, should you be faced with this dilemma, resist the urge to veer blindly from your path; rather, evaluate the terms of the deal, the gains, and the losses; identify your needs. Only then negotiate a good way to ensure that both you and your employer get what you need.

It is important to keep in mind that ACF certification is designed to help you develop your career. As pointed out in earlier chapters, the program has been revised many times over the years, always with the changes to our industry in mind. As you know by now, it supports several ways of measuring a given candidate based on job experience, knowledge, and a practical evaluation of skills. If, as a young cook, you read the information pertinent to each level, and incorporate it as a milestone on your career path, you will discover that the progress from level to level makes good sense: it is constructed to move you logically to executive chef or pastry chef. Each level requires a certain level of knowledge growth and skill sets, along with continuing improvement and development in the fundamentals.

To help you better understand the aspects of a cook's career, the following list summarizes the food knowledge a cook will need to be successful.

- *The foods we eat: developing all available foodstuffs.* As cooks, we have innumerable foodstuffs to work with. This presents us with one of our greatest challenges and one of our greatest pleasures. The study of food, which should never stop, can also be a fantastic source of entertainment. Food products are vastly different from region to region, country to country, and continent to continent, and cooks must become intimately familiar with as many different types of food and foodservice as possible in order to increase their understanding and to know how to pick the best available products.
- *Fundamentals of cookery:* This is a big category, and probably the most important, as most of the knowledge in it requires constant updating to remain proficient throughout our careers. The fundamentals encompass sanitation, nutrition, and the methods of cookery, along with all their subsets. As chefs we have a responsibility to our customers, first and foremost, to feed them in a sanitary, nutritious way. This is not to imply that we must become antiseptic food producers, but that we must at all times

consider the health of our guests. We must understand, respect, and know how to apply the information from the medical and dietary communities, while satisfying our customers and employers. And we must keep abreast of new information that comes from these sources.

Our greatest challenge in this category is to develop a thorough knowledge of how heat affects food and the standard ways to apply heat to food. Fortunately, there are many valuable sources of information available to us, and we should take advantage of them all. Once we have a basic "book learning," we must then begin to learn how to execute this knowledge. And make no mistake, it takes years to become proficient in this skill. It also takes a passion for the art of cooking—but that is another book! Perhaps the single most important part of this learning process is the involvement of your peers and mentors. In our craft there is no replacement for the hands of an older chef, one who has sautéed thousands of scaloppini or braised a million shanks. Skills attained over the years are invaluable, and, happily, most chefs are willing to share with their cooks.

THE GIFT OF SHARING

Sharing knowledge is at the very heart of the American Culinary Federation. So ask to be shown; seek out mentors. Absorb their knowledge; you will be the better for it. Do not rush this process; you will be the less for doing so.

- *Craftsmanship: making food ready for the heat.* All foods come in a package. As foodservice professionals, it is our task to understand the package, know how to take it apart, and then how to make it presentable and palatable. Mentoring is essential here as well, for there is much to learn about all the available foods and the many ways to prepare them for cooking.

You will start your quest for this knowledge by executing all the standards and by gaining experience in the many processes. This will not come easily, yet must be accomplished quickly. Practice is the key here. For example, when you first learn how to remove the parts of a chicken, it will seem quite laborious and probably take you 15 minutes to execute; but once you understand the system, you will be able to do it in around 2 minutes. Likewise, when you first try to ice a cake with whipped cream, it may turn to butter; but with practice you will produce a perfectly smooth, beautiful cake—quickly. And your developed competencies will directly relate to the certification testing mandates.

■ *Flavor and textural understanding: bringing the many aspects of foods together.* Once we know how to prepare food palatably, we must then learn to enhance it, using *complementary* foods—what goes with what. Involving creativity and an understanding of both food flavors and textures, this is another of the many challenging tasks of food preparation. Just determining what is "good" is a major undertaking, as there are almost as many definitions of "good" as there are cooks/chefs and customers. Is "good" what our customers want, or is it what the most discerning gastronomes of our time regard as correctly prepared food? Needless to say, these could be widely different concepts. In the face of this disparity, the chef is charged with deciding what the character of a dish will be, and then accomplishing that goal, by melding the various attributes of the foods and rendering it enjoyable. When it comes to certification testing, the bottom line is: the food must taste "good."

THE FUNDAMENTALS OF COMPOSITION

In order to gain knowledge about the fundamentals of composition, you are advised at some point during your education to seek out a course in basic visual understanding. This is usually referred to in a first-year art major curriculum as Visual Fundamentals or some equivalent. This type of a course should exhibit the fundamentals of visual perception through painting, sculpture, or drawing techniques. Many times it will be based on a rudimentary study of art history, and it should last about two semesters.

■ *Visual awareness: presenting the food in an appetizing fashion.* This may be as simple as serving a beautifully baked slice of apple pie with a round scoop of melting vanilla ice cream on top, or as complex as the "artworks" presented at world culinary competitions. Regardless of the level of complexity, what matters in the end is how the dish is perceived visually by the recipient. Therefore, all cooks and chefs should, at least fundamentally, understand visual composition—that is to say, the way people perceive the various arrangements of line, shape, and color, the foundations of all we see. To that end, there are some very specific rules to learn, which relate to the human perception of line, shape, and color, in conjunction with placement that facilitates the consumption of the foods and the retention of proper temperature. Once learned, the chef can apply them to every dish he or she presents on plate or platter. Without this formal training, chefs will struggle to frame their "artwork" to be visually appealing.

- *Refinement: honing skills to an advanced level.* The chef's next challenge is to hone his or her skills according to the requirements of the career path he or she is on. Put another way, the chef's basic skills should become almost second nature. It is like learning to drive a car: if after 10 years of driving, you still must think about the basics of operating the vehicle, chances are you will have a lot of fender benders—or worse! When a chef's skills have become virtually automatic, he or she is probably ready to move to a new level of mastery.

- *Management: bringing it all together.* Typically, with cooking skills mastered, a chef will move away from the range full time and begin to run a business. Of course, the skills to do this also have been nurtured along the career path: learning and understanding about food and labor costs, how to manage people, and how a business works and what is important to its success. It goes without saying that the specifics of each business will differ, but as in all other aspects of the foodservice profession, a basic fundamental skill set is the foundation for proficiency. For certification, practical evaluation of this skill set is through operational efficiency, professionalism, and the overall management capabilities of the candidate.

 ## CONCLUSION

As with any profession, if you want to achieve career success in the culinary field, you really need to know, understand, and develop the skill sets described previously. They provide a solid foundation on which culinary careers are based. Culinarians need to have a set of specific skills involving a blend science, art, people, and business proficiencies. It is a tough blend to master, and to be proficient in each of these areas takes a great deal of effort and study.

The culinary industry changes rapidly. So, you need to plan on continuing education along with carefully planned career development; both are necessities in order for you to reach your full potential. ACF Certification is designed to help you understand how to benchmark your successes and abilities with professional recognition at each turn. You must take the lead and monitor your own progress, develop self-challenges, and strive for your career goals, all the while recording your progress.

CHAPTER

6

Documenting Your Experience

YOUR LIFE AS A CULINARIAN WILL SOMETIMES SEEM TO MOVE WITH THE SPEED AND FURY OF A CLASS-FIVE HURRICANE, yet you must be able to track it as an organized progression. From the time you first "ride the range" until you have closed the walk-in for the last time, it is vitally important to maintain a history of your work experiences, awards, activities, education, and anything else related to your career. You're no doubt thinking this means the usual curriculum vitae or résumé, but that's only part of it. For the purpose of your certification "package," you will also need documentation—proof—of each statement of completion you make regarding ACF requirements.

THE PROOF IS IN THE DOCUMENTATION

Documentation of work experience or education can usually be accomplished by a few methods:

- A personally sworn and notarized statement as to your activity or work experience
- Proof of earnings, such as your paycheck stub or W-4 (always keep at the very least, the first and last paycheck stub of each place of employment)
- Official transcripts from educational institutions
- Statement on letterhead from businesses or organizations still in operation verifying your dates of employment and positions held
- Any document verifiable by phone or letter from the original source, such as a letter from employers or pertaining to your involvement with an event

In addition, make it a habit to start and maintain a list of any important special activities you participate in, such as philanthropic dinners or events you have helped with or any special cooking activities that are outside of your normal work realm. Similarly, keep track of any school activities that relate to your career, such as participation on student cooking teams, membership in relevant activity groups or clubs, and involvement in any culinary-related special events. And don't forget to make note of all your ACF activities: offices held, committee positions, and proof of attendance at ACF regional conferences and national conventions, along with any CE hours you accumulate. Along with your own personal record, it is advisable to obtain a letter from the source of the activity to corroborate your involvement. This proof should be created on the letterhead of the primary organization for the event.

Whenever you leave a place of employment, don't walk out the door without a signed letter stating your date of hire and final date of employment; and make sure it's on letterhead with contact information for the person signing the document. Often, if you prepare this letter yourself and simply present it for signature, the process will be more efficient. But larger companies may have policies that state specifically who can issue this type of letter and what it should say. In this case, usually you'll seek help from the human resources department to obtain the correct documentation.

ORGANIZING, PROTECTING, AND STORING DOCUMENTATION

Once you have organized yourself and developed collection techniques that work for you, you must figure out the most effective way to organize, protect, and store your professional experience documentation. In doing so, you need to consider how to safeguard it from damage or loss, yet make sure you have what you need when you need it. Here are some suggestions:

- For storage, buy a fireproof safe, one rated to withstand temperatures of 350 degrees for at least two hours.
- Scan or otherwise duplicate all documents electronically and store them in two separate places, such as at home in the aforementioned safe and at work. Use one of the readily available and inexpensive portable digital storage devices.
- Burn all documents onto two CD-ROMs, and store each in a separate place.
- Enclose all original paper documents in an acid-free portfolio, remembering to remove all staples and paperclips (which can damage paper over time), then put it in the fire safe.
- Make photocopies of paper documentation and keep them in two different places.

All these in and of themselves are good practices, but better yet is to utilize more than one.

CONCLUSION

The key to maintaining your work-related documentation is to stay on top of the process. When you do, it is reasonably simple; when you don't, you'll find yourself in a bind when you need up-to-date documentation at a moment's notice for whatever reason. And when it comes to storing documents, think the unthinkable: fire, acts of nature, and vandalism do occur, and if they do, you want to have the backup you need to minimize the damage and save you precious time.

CHAPTER

7

Levels of ACF Certification

THERE ARE CURRENTLY 14 LEVELS OF ACF CERTIFICATION designated for professional cooks, chefs, and culinary educators. Each is designed to represent one step in a professional culinarian's typical career path, which could lead to various specializations, among them baking and pastry, education, and administration. And for each level there are specific qualifying requirements, all of which lead to and support the requirements for subsequent, higher, levels of certification. Ideally, a young culinarian will begin his or her professional career as a Certified Culinarian or Pastry Culinarian and reach the pinnacle as a Master Chef or Master Pastry Chef. Certainly, this is an achievable goal for those who choose to pursue it.

ACF LEVELS OF ACHIEVEMENT

Whether you are applying for certification for the first time or are planning your next step up the ACF career ladder, the certification levels help define each stage of professional development in the foodservice industry; hence, they can be used as a guide to your personal successes. Each step is, then, a milestone; more specifically, each new level signals a major change in knowledge, experience, and responsibilities, which, taken together, define the structure of professional kitchen organizations.

So that you may fully understand the ACF certification levels, review the job descriptions for each, given in the following sections. Then identify where you are currently on your career path so that you can determine how to proceed to reach your ultimate professional destination.

FOR MORE INFORMATION

For more details on certification levels, contact the ACF national office at 800-624-9458 or visit their Web site at www.acfchefs.org.

Culinarian

A culinarian is an entry-level culinary professional in a commercial foodservice operation, responsible for preparing and cooking sauces, cold foods, fish, soups and stocks, meats, vegetables, eggs, and other food items. Job titles that qualify for this designation include:

- Cook
- Line cook
- Station cook
- Broiler cook
- Sauté cook
- Fry cook

Certified Culinarians (CCs) need a minimum of three years of documented full-time work experience in a variety of culinary production positions. They are educated in the fundamentals of math, science, communications, culinary arts, food safety, nutrition, management, teamwork and cultural diversity.

A typical Certified Culinarian is a high school graduate with specialized training and further education in culinary arts. The majority are graduates of two- or four-year culinary arts programs and/or ACF apprenticeship programs.

Pastry Culinarian

This is an entry-level culinary professional in the baking and/or pastry area of a foodservice operation. He or she is responsible for the preparation and production of pies, cookies, cakes, breads, rolls, desserts, and other baked goods. Job titles that qualify for this designation include:

- Baker
- Baker's assistant
- Pastry cook
- Pastry assistant

Certified Pastry Culinarians (CPCs) have a minimum of three years of documented full-time work experience in a variety of baking and/or pastry production positions. They are educated in the fundamentals of math, science, communications, baking arts, food safety, nutrition, management, teamwork, and cultural diversity.

A typical Certified Pastry Culinarian is a high school graduate with specialized training and further education in baking arts. The majority are graduates of two- or four-year culinary/pastry arts programs and/or ACF pastry cook apprenticeship programs.

Personal Chef

A personal chef is engaged in the preparation, cooking, and serving of foods on a "cook-for-hire" basis in private residences. He or she is responsible for menu planning, development, marketing, and culinary, financial, and operational management of private business; he or she also provides cooking services to a variety of clients. Job titles that qualify for this designation include:

61

- Personal chef
- Catering chef
- Residence chef
- Private home chef

Personal Certified Chefs (PCCs) have a minimum of four years of professional cooking experience, with a minimum of one full year employed as a personal chef. They are educated in the fundamentals of math, science, communications, cooking and baking arts, food safety, nutrition, menu planning, business management, and customer relations.

A typical Personal Certified Chef is a high school graduate with specialized training and further education in cooking, baking, and business management. The majority are graduates of two- or four-year culinary/pastry arts and/or hospitality management programs.

Sous Chef

A sous chef is considered second in charge in a foodservice operation, reporting directly to the executive chef or chef de cuisine. Sous chefs often supervise an entire shift by themselves and fill the position of the executive chef in his or her absence. Sous chef is the first supervisory position a cook might have.

For ACF certification sous chefs must supervise a minimum of two full-time people in the preparation of food. Job titles that qualify for this designation include:

- Sous chef
- Banquet chef
- Garde-manger chef
- Day (A.M.) chef and evening (P.M.) chef

Certified Sous Chefs (CSCs) have at least two years of experience as a sous chef supervising two or more people and a minimum of three additional years of progressive culinary work experience. They are educated in the fundamentals of math, science, communications, cooking and baking arts, food safety, nutrition, supervision, management, teamwork, and cultural diversity.

A typical Certified Sous Chef is a high school graduate with specialized training and further education in cooking, baking, supervision, and management. The majority are graduates of two- or four-year culinary arts programs and/or ACF apprenticeship programs.

Working Pastry Chef

This is a pastry culinarian responsible for a pastry section or a shift within a foodservice operation, bakery, or pastry shop. He or she has considerable responsibility for the preparation and production of pies, cookies, cakes, breads, rolls, desserts, confections, and other baked goods. Job titles that qualify for this position include:

- Lead baker
- A.M. or P.M. pastry chef
- Pastry Sous Chef

Certified Working Pastry Chefs (CWPCs) have at least two years of experience as a pastry chef, with a minimum of three additional years of progressive baking and pastry work experience. They are educated in the fundamentals of math, science, communications, baking and pastry arts, food safety, nutrition, supervision, management, teamwork, and cultural diversity.

A typical Certified Working Pastry Chef is a high school graduate with specialized training and further education in baking, pastry, supervision, and management. The majority are graduates of two- or four-year culinary arts programs and/or ACF pastry cook apprenticeship programs.

Chef de Cuisine

This chef is the supervisor in charge of food production in a foodservice operation, which could mean a single unit of a multiunit operation or a freestanding operation. He or she is, in essence, the chef of this operation, with final decision-making power as it relates to culinary operations. The person in this position must supervise a minimum of three full-time people in the production of food. Normally, the chef de cuisine reports to a corporate chef, food and beverage director, or owner. Job titles that qualify for this designation include:

- Chef
- Chef de cuisine
- Executive sous chef
- Catering chef
- Banquet chef (in larger operations)

Certified Chefs de Cuisine (CCCs) have at least three years of experience as the lead chef or chef de cuisine, with a minimum of three additional years of progressive cooking and sous chef experience. They are educated in the fundamentals of math, science, communications, cooking, baking, food safety, nutrition, supervision, management, menu planning, teamwork, and cultural diversity.

A typical Certified Chef de Cuisine is a high school graduate with a significant amount of additional education and specialized training in cooking, baking, supervision, and management. The majority are graduates of two- or four-year culinary arts programs and/or ACF apprenticeship programs.

Secondary Culinary Educator

A secondary culinary educator is an advanced-degreed professional who is working as an educator in an accredited secondary or vocational institution and is responsible for the development, implementation, administration, evaluation, and maintenance of a culinary arts or foodservice management curriculum. Job titles that qualify for this designation include:

- Culinary instructor
- Chef instructor

Certified Secondary Culinary Educators (CSCEs) have at least two years of experience as a high school or vocational school instructor, with a minimum of three additional years of progressive teaching, cooking, and/or baking experience. They are educated in the fundamentals of education, math, science, communications, cooking, baking, food safety, nutrition, supervision, teamwork, and cultural diversity.

A typical Certified Secondary Culinary Educator has a bachelor's degree, with a major in, for example, culinary arts, hospitality management, education, education development, or vocational education. Some may even have a master's degree and a doctorate in management and/or educational concentrations.

Culinary Educator

A culinary educator is an advanced-degreed culinary professional who is working as an educator in an accredited postsecondary institution or military training facility. He or she is responsible for the development, implementation, administration, evaluation, and maintenance of a culinary arts or foodservice management curriculum. Job titles that qualify for this designation include:

- Culinary instructor
- Chef instructor
- Culinary lecturer
- Associate culinary instructor
- Professor of culinary education

Certified Culinary Educators (CCEs) have at least two years of experience as a culinary educator, teaching cooking- and baking-related courses in a professional culinary arts education program for an accredited institution of higher learning. In addition, they have a minimum of three years of progressive professional cooking and/or baking experience, including supervisory positions. They possess superior culinary experience and expertise, equivalent to that of the Certified Chef de Cuisine or Certified Working Pastry Chef.

A typical Certified Culinary Educator has a bachelor's degree, with a major in culinary arts, hospitality management, education, education development, or vocational education. Some also have a master's degree and/or a doctorate in management or educational concentrations.

Personal Executive Chef

This chef has advanced culinary skills, provides cooking services on a "cook-for-hire-basis" to a variety of clients, and is responsible for menu planning and development and for making marketing, financial management, and operational decisions. He or she is also expected to provide nutritious and safe foods that are visually appealing, properly flavored, and delicious. Job titles that qualify for this designation include:

- Personal chef
- Catering chef
- Residence chef
- Private home chef

Personal Certified Executive Chefs (PCECs) have a minimum of six years of professional cooking experience, including a minimum of two full years as a personal chef. They are educated in the fundamentals of math, science, communications, cooking and baking arts, food safety, nutrition, menu planning, business management, and customer relations.

A typical Personal Certified Executive Chef is a high school graduate with a significant amount of additional education and specialized training in cooking, baking, supervision, and business management. The majority are graduates of two- or four-year culinary arts programs and/or ACF apprenticeship programs.

Executive Pastry Chef

An executive pastry chef is a department head, usually reporting to the executive chef of a foodservice operation, food and beverage director, or owner. He or she is in complete charge of baking and pastry planning and production for the operation, ensuring that all bakery and pastry products produced meet or exceed company standards. Job titles that qualify for this designation include:

- Pastry chef
- Executive pastry chef
- Head pastry chef

Certified Executive Pastry Chefs (CEPCs) have at least five years of experience as the lead pastry chef in a professional bakery or pastry production facility, restaurant, club, or hotel, with a minimum of three additional years of progressive baking and pastry experience. They are educated in the fundamentals of math, science, communications, cooking, baking, pastry, food safety, nutrition, supervision, management, menu planning, teamwork, and cultural diversity.

A typical Certified Executive Pastry Chef is a high school graduate with a significant amount of additional education and specialized training in cooking, baking, pastry production, supervision, and management. The majority are graduates of two- or four-year culinary/pastry arts programs and/or ACF pastry apprenticeship programs.

Executive Chef

The executive chef is the department head responsible for all culinary units in a restaurant, hotel, club, hospital, or other foodservice establishment. He or she might also be the owner of a foodservice operation. The executive chef reports to management and coordinates responsibilities and activities with other departments. Other duties include menu planning, budget preparation, payroll, maintenance, controlling food costs, and maintaining financial and inventory records. He or she must possess a basic knowledge of food safety and sanitation, culinary nutrition, and supervisory management. Job titles that qualify for this designation include:

- Head chef
- Executive chef
- Kitchen manager
- Catering manager
- Chef de cuisine (of some large operations)

Certified Executive Chefs (CECs) have a minimum of five years of experience as an executive chef, with a minimum of five to six years of experience in progressive culinary positions. They must supervise a minimum of five full-time persons in the production and service of food. They are educated in the fundamentals of math, science, communications, cooking, baking, pastry, food safety, nutrition, supervision, management, menu planning, teamwork, and cultural diversity.

A typical Certified Executive Chef is a high school graduate with a significant amount of additional education and specialized training in cooking, baking, supervision, and business management. The majority are graduates of two- or four-year culinary/pastry arts programs and/or ACF apprenticeship programs. Some may have a bachelor's or master's degree or a doctorate in a variety of disciplines.

Culinary Administrator

This is an executive-level chef who is responsible for the administrative functions of running a professional foodservice operation. To qualify for this certification, this culinary professional must demonstrate proficiency in culinary knowledge, human resources, operational management, and business planning skills. Job titles that qualify for this designation include:

- Culinary administrator
- Corporate chef
- Culinary director

Certified Culinary Administrators (CCAs) have a minimum of five years of experience as a culinary administrator, with a minimum of five to six additional years in progressive culinary positions with supervision experience. They must supervise a minimum of 10 full-time-equivalent employees. They are educated in the fundamentals of math, science, communications, cooking, baking, food safety, nutrition, supervision, menu planning, and strategic, financial, and personnel management.

A typical Certified Culinary Administrator has a minimum of an associate's degree in culinary arts or hospitality management, with specialized training in cooking, baking, supervision, and business management. The majority are graduates of two- or four-year culinary/pastry arts programs and/or ACF apprenticeship programs. Many have bachelor's or master's degrees or doctorates in a variety of business and/or hospitality management disciplines.

Master Chef/Master Pastry Chef

This is the consummate chef, one who possesses a high degree of professional culinary knowledge, skills, and experience. He or she teaches and supervises the entire crew, as well as provides leadership and serves as a role model for younger culinarians. Many ACF Certified Master Chefs/Pastry Chefs find jobs in the most exclusive operations around the world, including high-scale country clubs, as corporate chefs, corporate research chefs, and foodservice/hospitality consultants.

Certification as a CEC or CEPC is a prerequisite to applying for ACF Master Chef/Pastry Chef certification. Candidates must meet and exceed the minimum culinary and professional standards of executive chefs/pastry chefs and demonstrate proficiency in classical and world cuisines.

There is no typical Certified Master Chef/Pastry Chef (CMC/CMPC) portfolio. Many of today's ACF Certified Master Chefs/Pastry Chefs were educated in European culinary career colleges and universities, earned their professional certifications abroad, and served their apprenticeships there. However, since 1980, a growing number of American trained and educated chefs are earning the titles of Certified Master Chef and/or Certified Master Pastry Chef.

CONCLUSION

The ACF certification ladder allows culinarians to earn recognition for their expertise at whatever level of professional development they may find themselves. Whether starting out as young culinarians or entering the certification process well into their careers, culinarians can find an ACF certification level that matches their level of expertise as well as another, higher level to which they can aspire.

When a culinarian's education and experience increases, so too does her or his self-worth and value to employers. ACF certification is a way of displaying those professional accomplishments in terms the industry can understand.

The ACF Written Test: Strategies in Learning

THE ACF IMPLEMENTED WRITTEN EXAMS AS PART OF ITS CERTIFI-
CATION PROGRAM early in the history of the program as a means
to measure each candidate's general knowledge of cooking, baking, and kitchen management. Since then, the ACF certification
exams have evolved into a series of measurement tools that help
to determine the level of comprehension among culinarians on
the subjects that affect every aspect of their working lives. The
exams are designed to reflect the level of competency expected
by the industry of those who bear the titles of Certified
Culinarian through the highest level of Certified Master Chef.

The exams are not intended to measure one's mastery of the
subjects, as you might expect in a formal college testing environment, but to prove general culinary knowledge by testing on
myriad subjects based on thousands of questions and possible
answers. The tests are not intended to fail applicants, but to
prove what they know.

WHO TAKES THE ACF CERTIFIED EXAMS?

Naturally, everyone applying for ACF professional certifications takes the exam appropriate for the level of certification they are applying for, hoping to pass them as part of the application requirements; but others take the exams for various personal and professional reasons.

Here is a short list of other reasons for taking nationally recognized competency exams like the ACF's level-specific certification exams:

- To screen applicants applying for new jobs at various positions
- To measure an existing employee's readiness to be promoted to a higher rank
- To measure one's own level of competency to be better able to plan for the next step in a career path
- To ensure one's confidence that he or she has the broad-based culinary knowledge required for progressive culinary careers

Certification applicants are advised to take the exam after they have completed their mandatory courses (Sanitation, Nutrition, and Supervisory Management) or the refresher courses (eight hours every five years on the same subjects), because the exams contain questions regarding them. Those types of questions are detailed-oriented, such as:

- What is the proper temperature for serving pork?
- What are the differences between fat and water-soluble vitamins?
- What is meant by Theory X and Theory Y types of employees?

These questions ask for very specific pieces of information that can only be learned from a legitimate reference, textbook, or class. By studying these courses first, each candidate can improve his or her chances of succeeding the first time through.

Scores for certification exams are valid for up to two years after they are taken, or until significant changes are made to the testing methodologies, matrixes, and/or questions they contain. The written and practical cooking/baking exams (where required) should be the last two items candidates complete before submitting their application to ensure their acceptability.

Many culinarians will also take "practice" certification tests, to test their readiness for certification. If they pass the exam, then they are one step closer to being certified. If they do not pass the exam the first time through, they can go back and study the areas of the test they are deficient in and retake the exam with great confidence when they are ready to apply.

WHO ADMINISTERS THE TESTS?

The tests are administered by a national computer testing agency to ensure easy access by candidates throughout the United States. Information about the current provider for certification tests is on the ACF Web site (www.acfchefs.org) or by calling the ACF national office (800-624-9458). Currently, ACF certification exams are being administered by LaserGrade, LLC, which operates more than 1,000 test centers in or near most major airports and other metropolitan landmarks in all 50 states.

The tests are proctored by trained personnel who ensure that they are duly taken by each candidate using the most discrete and secure procedures possible. The testing proctor also ensures that the computers the candidates use to access the tests are working properly and that the area assigned for taking the test is secured, quiet, and well lit at all times. No materials can be brought into the room while the candidates take their exams. In most cases, video cameras or mirrors are used to protect against interferences to the test-taking process.

Identification cards and/or state-issued driver licenses are required proof of identity before taking the exams.

THE EXAM MATRIX

The ACF Certification exam database contains more than 5,000 culinary-related questions in 12 major categories of topic areas representing hundreds of individual knowledge competencies. Each test is created one at a time by a sophisticated testing management program, which draws questions randomly from preassigned categories of topic areas according to the matrix the ACF certification committee has set for each level of certification.

These matrixes set the ratio or percentages of questions drawn from each category so that each level of certification test represents the knowledge associated with that level of cooking, baking, teaching, and/or culinary administration. The category of questions and the percentage of questions drawn from them change with each level of test and expand into more advanced topics for higher levels of certification.

As discussed in Chapter 3, the 12 categories of test questions are:

- Basic cooking
- Basic baking
- Advanced cooking
- Advanced baking/pastry
- Nutrition/nutritional cooking
- Sanitation and food safety
- Supervisory management
- Education development
- Education psychology (CSCE, CCE only)
- Business planning
- Human resources (CCA only)
- Operational management (CCA only)

Table 1 itemizes the current test matrixes used for each certification level. Note the variance as the position increases in authority and responsibilities.

REFERENCE MATERIALS

Each category of test has more than 400 questions drawn from various approved sources, including ACF's own collection of textbooks, videos, and training manuals. Great care is taken not

TABLE 1   ACF Test Matrixes

Certified Culinarian	Certified Pastry Culinarian	Personal Certified Chef	Certified Sous Chef
60% Basic Cooking 10% Sanitation 10% Nutrition 10% Supervisory Management 10% Basic Baking	60% Basic Baking 10% Sanitation 10% Nutrition 10% Supervisory Management 10% Basic Cooking	35% Basic Cooking 15% Advanced Cooking 15% Sanitation 15% Nutrition 10% Business Planning 10% Basic Baking	35% Basic Cooking 15% Advanced Cooking 15% Sanitation 15% Nutrition 10% Supervisory Management 10% Basic Baking

Certified Working Pastry Chef	Certified Chef de Cuisine	Certified Secondary Culinary Educator	Certified Culinary Educator
40% Basic Baking 20% Advanced Baking 10% Basic Cooking 10% Sanitation 10% Nutrition 10% Supervisory Management	25% Basic Cooking 20% Advanced Cooking 15% Supervisory Management 15% Sanitation 15% Nutrition 10% Basic Baking	20% Education Development 15% Sanitation 15% Nutrition 10% Supervisory Management 15% Basic Baking 25% Basic Cooking	20% Education Development 15% Sanitation 15% Nutrition 10% Supervisory Management 10% Basic Baking 5% Advanced Baking 15% Advanced Cooking 10% Basic Cooking

Personal Certified Executive Chef	Certified Executive Pastry Chef	Certified Executive Chef	Certified Culinary Administrator
25% Advanced Cooking 15% Sanitation 15% Nutrition 15% Business Planning 15% Basic Cooking 10% Basic Baking 5% Advanced Baking	25% Advanced Baking 20% Basic Baking 15% Sanitation 15% Nutrition 15% Supervisory Management 10% Basic Cooking	25% Advanced Cooking 15% Sanitation 15% Nutrition 15% Supervisory Management 15% Basic Cooking 10% Basic Baking 5% Advanced Baking	Must take a business exam in addition to taking the CEC exam for the culinary competencies.

(continues)

TABLE 1   ACF Test Matrixes *(Continued)*

Business Exam
40% Human Resources 40% Operational Management 20% Business Planning

to pull questions directly from the texts unless they are considered to be "general knowledge."

General knowledge can be defined as information that has been validated by multiple sources, or is "generally" believed to be true and accurate. Book authors tend to inflect their own personal beliefs and philosophies in their writing, and it is this aspect that should never make it onto a test paper. Testing is not a measurement of one's ability to memorize, but of general knowledge on each particular subject.

This is especially true with cooking and baking texts where recipes are involved. One author might make a claim for certain items or techniques to be used in a particular recipe, while another author might not agree. Does that make one author right and the other one wrong, or just indicate an interpretation of the dish itself? Interpretations as well as ideas and personal beliefs should not be part of any test, let alone the ACF certification tests. Therefore, recipes are not used to configure test questions except what is drawn from Escoffier, as mentioned in earlier chapters.

Many professionally published two-year college-level culinary and baking textbooks make adequate study guides for the certification exams. Because the questions are not textbook-specific, any generally well-recognized text or series of texts would offer each candidate a good solid starting point from which to study. There are not as many nationally recognized sanitation, nutrition, or supervisory management books to choose from, but taking the mandatory courses prior to testing should accommodate all the information that is needed in those three areas.

Escoffier's Complete Guide to the Art of Modern Cookery (*Le Guide Culinaire*) is used as a reference for many of the advanced cooking questions pertinent to the Certified Sous Chef and higher levels of certification. The tests, however, reference only the first two sections of the book, which include all the information on stocks, roux, and sauces, and the various garnishes that are used to define many classical preparations. These are the sections that still pertain to everyday professional cooking experience, and still maintain their value in the modern kitchen. Astute culinarians will want to study the entire work, for it is full of recipes and procedures unmatched by any other publication of its kind to this date.

Candidates for Certified Working Pastry Chef and Executive Pastry Chef should also study from a recognized pastry textbook, one that takes the student beyond the scope of basic baking into the whole world of pastry and fine decorated cakes/ tortes. Here, too, the questions are not recipe-specific, but each working pastry chef and/or executive pastry chef must have a broader scope of knowledge than the typical culinary/baking school graduate can learn in only two years.

Sacher Torte, for example, is a very specific type of torte made from chocolate genoise and raspberry jam and coated with a poured chocolate icing. Pound cake is another, albeit more simple, example. Any number of books might list the ingredients differently, but everyone around the globe should know that every pound cake is made primarily from eggs, fat, flour, and sugar (originally, one pound of each of these ingredients were used, thus the name "pound cake"). While a test question would not ask for specific ingredients for any single recipe, it could refer to nationally known pastry products and the flavors and components that make them what they are. Other examples might be: Charlotte Russe (molded Bavarian cream surrounded by ladyfingers), Linzer Tort (a pielike filled cookie made with ground hazelnuts and raspberry preserves), and Black Forest Cake (chocolate genoise filled with a tart cherry filling flavored with Kirshwasser [cherry brandy], iced with whipped cream, and garnished with pitted tart cherries).

Candidates for Certified Educator (secondary and postsecondary) should refer to any number of general teaching methodologies textbooks to study for their exam. These candidates should already be familiar with teaching strategies and techniques, including curriculum development, assessments, and education psychology, but they may need to refresh their memories by referencing one or more contemporary teaching books. Again, the questions pertaining to education and education development are general information questions. Most teacher training programs and in-service programs regularly touch on the subjects contained in the exam. A competent instructor with a few years of professional teaching experience should be able to answer the education questions without much additional study.

The newest certification to be added to the ACF ladder is Certified Culinary Administrator (CCA). This high-level culinary position is more regularly responsible for the management and business operation of foodservice operations than the cooking line. Candidates should be able to demonstrate a higher level of business proficiencies, as well as a foundation in culinary knowledge. It is recommended that candidates for CCA study texts on general business topics such as strategic, financial, and personnel management.

STUDY TO ACHIEVE SUCCESS

No test worth taking should be passable without some amount of study or practice. The same is true of the ACF written and practical cooking/baking exams. If certification candidates could simply walk off the street and pass their certification exam it would suggest that the exams were not comprehensive enough to measure even the basic understanding of related knowledge. Study of the materials and practice of the skills is imperative to the success of each candidate attempting certification.

This is not to say that most professionals applying for the certifications have difficulty performing their jobs because of a lack of understanding of basic terms and techniques, but that the details of what they should know often escapes their memories when it comes to taking the tests. Especially for seasoned professional cooks and chefs who have not been in an academic setting for many years, taking tests can be stressful and complicated. Study and practice refreshes knowledge and skills, as well as one's confidence in his or her own abilities to get the job done.

Study and practice are the two best methods for passing the ACF exams. When each candidate succeeds, he or she can be proud to know that he or she truly achieved something and was not simply handed a title because of a job or position. Certified cooks and chefs are *educated and skilled* cooks and chefs.

CHAPTER

9

Evaluating Cooking Skills: The Premise behind the Practical Exam

ONCE A CHEF OR COOK HAS DECIDED TO BECOME CERTIFIED, he or she has a number of goals to accomplish. This chapter and the next address the one most cooks find the most intimidating: the practical exam. Here's the scenario:

1. You go to an unfamiliar kitchen.
2. You are observed by a group of evaluators while you work on a program of required competencies.
3. The group evaluates the finished items.
4. You enter into a discussion, known as the "critique," about your performance, at the end of which you learn whether or not you have succeeded.

It is not uncommon during this test for even the most confident of chefs to be nervous and feel uncertain. Tasks that chefs routinely and competently accomplish every day of their working lives suddenly feel like brand-new challenges. The result is that some chefs fail to perform at their best. By knowing this in advance, you can prepare, by understanding thoroughly what will be expected of you. Doing so will reduce the potential anxiety, enabling you to perform at the top of your game. And even if you fail in this attempt the first time, take heart: pay careful attention to the critique, correct your mistakes, and try again.

MIND-SET FOR SUCCESS

The ACF practical exam is a sound process that does a good job of assessing a cook's skill level. In this section we will describe that process in brief, to help you get into the mind-set to be evaluated and critiqued, so that you may successfully achieve the level of certification you desire.

The first rule of the game is simple, so simple it can be said in one word: practice . . . or you will most likely fail. Too often, unfortunately, chefs fail to heed this advice. We as chefs are creatures of habit and must function within a routine. If you practice your routine, chances are you will succeed.

To pass the practical exam you will have to demonstrate that you understand the numerous individual capabilities that, when added together, amount to the sum total of a professional cook. When you submit yourself to an evaluation of your skills in a practical setting, you are, in essence, saying, "I have the skill set to be certified at the level for which I am testing, and I would like the team of evaluators to document that assertion." The evaluators will make their determination based on a series of predetermined guidelines, which require you to perform a lengthy set of competencies, each of which gives you the opportunity to demonstrate your proficiency at that particular skill. These are iterative tasks leading to the final result and are considered subsets of your overall competency, all affecting the final evaluation. Each competency is awarded points, which, taken together, will add up to the final determination of competency. (More about this topic will be said in Chapter 10.)

UNDERSTANDING THE ROLE OF THE EVALUATORS

The role of the evaluators (there are three) sounds straightforward: to make a decision as to a candidate's success or failure on the practical exam. But it's much more complex, for they must base their decision on evidence that is not black and white; rather, it comprises a contiguous understanding of whether the candidate is accomplishing his or her stated goal.

To do this, in addition to fully understanding the parameters of the practical exam, the evaluators must rely on their own industry experience and knowledge to carefully rate all the activities of the candidate during the testing period (assigning each a score), relate them to the competency level, evaluate whether or not he or she is acceptable and at what level, then generate a final score. In doing so, the evaluators must also take into consideration the status of the candidate's career in relation to the particular skill, because it is reasonable to expect that craftsmanship and expertise grow with experience. Take the process of sautéing: whereas a young cook would be expected to understand and be able to execute the procedure, an executive chef would be expected to sauté as if it were second nature—and using a more complex set of ingredients and flavors.

Candidates need to realize that as they climb the certification ladder their understanding and demonstration of the cooking processes increases incrementally. The learning process generated by this exercise is one of the core purposes of certification. As culinarians become certified, they not only achieve self-fulfillment but they force themselves to learn and grow. They are also making a strong testimonial that certification is important to our industry and should be sought. The process is meant to raise the level of professionalism through education and the understanding of our craft. Consequently, by submitting yourself to the program you will need to gain a solid understanding of cooking processes, sanitation, methodology, flavor construction, and organization. Perhaps this all sounds intimidating; after all, it is a great deal of information. However it is all based on and encompasses the knowledge a professional chef or pastry chef needs to have. Keep in mind: The bench-

83

mark for the level of understanding in order to succeed is set at a minimum to achieve each level of certification.

As you can see, the evaluators of the practical exam shoulder a great responsibility, both to the individual candidates and the profession at large. And there's more. In addition to the afore-mentioned, evaluators must approve and confirm that the test administrator has arranged the testing facility and process appropriately. In this regard, they are charged with ensuring the integrity of the exam and the timing and scheduling of the can-didates; they must verify that the facility meets all require-ments—that correct equipment is in place, that proper sanitation procedures have been implemented, that ample refrigeration is available, that vents are in working order, and that there is appropriate workspace. Initially, it is up to the test administra-tor to ensure that all these requirements are met, but it is the final responsibility of the examiner team to approve and con-firm what the administrator has arranged. In sum, the evaluator team serves as support for all candidates; they are there to resolve expeditiously any questions, problems, or concerns can-didates may have, so that nothing interferes with the candi-dates' performance. Evaluators will not, however, answer any questions or supply information that would help the candidate in regard to the competencies being tested.

Be aware that, during your exam, the evaluators will do a lot of note taking; don't let this make you nervous. It is necessary for three important reasons. First, notes enable the evaluator to keep track of your performance from start to finish in order to gen-erate an accurate score. Second, evaluators refer to these notes during the critique following the exam, to assure that they address all aspects of your performance. (If you have been successful, the cri-tique will focus on what you need to do to plan for the next level of certification or reinforce your positive activity.) And, third, the notes are used later as reference for the report evaluators must submit to the national office on your performance.

ON FILE

Documentation of unsuccess-ful certification test results is kept on file in the ACF's national office, where it is retained only for use in the grievance process; it is never released to any candidate.

I bring up the writing of notes because candidates can

become very nervous when in the presence of an evaluator who is standing at their station writing. This should not bother the candidate; it is necessary no matter whether your performance is good or unacceptable. I always would force myself to believe that the evaluator is writing about the previous candidate he visited!

CONCLUSION

When preparing for the practical exam, remember that where you are on the certification ladder will determine the expectation of your understanding of and ability to execute the cooking processes at incrementally higher levels. The learning process generated by this exercise is one of the core purposes of certification. By becoming certified, you not only are achieving professional recognition but are making a personal commitment to continue to learn and grow in your chosen field. You are also making a strong statement that certification is important to the industry, that it is something worth aspiring to. The process is meant to raise the level of professionalism through education and the understanding of our craft.

Taking the Show on the Road: More on the Practical Testing Process

IN CHAPTER 9, we touched on the importance of practicing for the practical certification exam. All chefs seeking certification and embarking on the certification process need to realize that the primary reason for practicing is to make the cumbersome activity of "taking the show on the road" just another process with which they become intimately familiar and comfortable.

For the practical exam, you will be going to an unfamiliar setting to produce foods under the watchful eyes of three evaluators who will judge your performance as either worthy of certification or not. To meet this challenge, you must carefully practice your whole production plan, as the decision to certify you will be based on your performance in this test. The evaluators will be looking for demonstrable skills that apply to the certification level you are seeking, and it is up to you to learn what that involves—that is, at what level you will need to perform to meet or exceed industry standards. Fortunately, the methodology for this is simple and age-old: seek out those who are experienced and ask them to share their knowledge. Historically, this required an often-harsh apprenticeship under a master craftsman; today, you need look no further than the ACF, the strongest network of talented, generous chefs in the world. The foundation of our federation is one of sharing with one another and helping each other to succeed.

Still, it is up to you to seek out those with experience and ask for assistance. Among those advisors, it is advisable to include senior chefs, educators, and others who have achieved certification, to help you understand your position and what you need to do to be successful. To get full value from this process, realize two things: it won't always be easy, and you won't always get the answer you want. For example, you may be tempted to assume that because you are employed in a certain position, and boast a title to match, that you have met all the requirements of that stage in your career. But consider: an executive chef working in a small restaurant may not have had the same industry exposure as an executive chef in a four-star hotel. Therefore, that small-restaurant chef may be forced to recognize that he or she has not had a broad enough experience to become a CEC. Conversely, the hotel chef may have to consider that because he or she has not been on the cooking line for five years, it will be very difficult for him or her to succeed at a cooking practical without first doing some intensive practice to refresh her skills. In neither case should the chef refrain from the attempt; rather, the self-assessment for both should serve to make the chef aware that he or she must approach the process correctly in order to be successful.

This example, for the purpose of this discussion, oversimplifies the situation, but nevertheless represents the variables involved in understanding your position and level of experience. It also makes the point that, more often than not, candidates who fail the practical exam are usually those who have not taken the time to practice.

PREPARING TO PREPARE

As implied in the foregoing, conducting a self-evaluation is the first step to a successful outcome of the practical exam; in short, it is paramount that you clearly understand both your professional strengths and weaknesses. A good way to proceed with this task is to:

1. Design a menu from the list of prescribed ingredients
2. Prepare a checklist containing each and every task of the practical process of preparing the menu
3. Going down the list, determine whether your skills are either "acceptable" or "unacceptable" in each category

To help you visualize this process, look at the menu shown in Figure 1 and the checklist shown in Figure 2. [Note that this example is for the Certified Executive Chef (CEC) level practical exam.]

The type of list shown in Figure 2 is easy to produce for your individual situation. Simply base it on your menu choice, which will quickly tell you most of the components needed to accomplish your goal, which is to produce a simple, flavorful meal that meets all of the mandated requirements of the test. Taking this

Pan-roasted Salmon and Braised Fennel
Shallow Poached Lobster Tail
Lemon Chive Sauce

∞

Mixed Greens
Basil-marinated Tomatoes, Bacon Crumbles,
and Crispy Onions
Green Apple Vinaigrette

∞

Sautéed Chicken Breast Scaloppini
Spinach and Artichoke Cake, Glazed Carrots,
and Rosemary Mashed Potatoes
Pan Sauce with Calamata Olives, Capers,
and Sweet Peppers

Figure 1   Menu for the CEC Level Practical Exam

Skills	Unacceptable	Acceptable
Sanitation		
Organization		
Ingredient utilization		
Skills		
Craftsmanship		
Serving methods		
Portion size understanding		
Flavor development		
Textural understanding		
Plate presentation		
Nutritional consciousness		
Methodologies		
Pan Roasting		
Vegetable braising		
Shallow poaching		
Lobster fabrication		
Sauce from cuisson		
Bacon bits		
Fried onions		
Emulsified vinaigrette		
Sauté		
Artichoke pairing		
Artichoke cookery		
Subric method		
Vegetable glazing		
Mashed potatoes		
Pan sauce from sauté		

Figure 2   Skills and Capabilities Checklist for CEC Practical Exam

personal skills inventory will dictate where you will spend most of your practice time and effort.

Getting Your Timing Right

Once you have developed your menu and the list of competencies appropriate to your level of certification, the next step is to begin practicing each element on the list until you are confident that your level of competency is acceptable.

During each stage of this process, be sure to involve both peers and mentors, as "practice evaluators." They will be able to give you an objective assessment of your work, which will help in two important ways: you will begin to understand the overriding framework of the practical, that is, the timing; and you will know when you are ready to practice the whole process within the constraints of the time frame.

COUNTING THE MINUTES
For the CEC practical exam, you will be given 195 minutes. There are varying time constraints depending on the level; however, the following exercise is applicable in concept to all exams. You should have no trouble meeting the time frame if you follow the practice guidelines given in this section.

We suggest that you practice each step, timing as you go, until you feel proficient; then draw up a timeline to plan your execution of the test as a single unit. Figure 3 gives an example of a timeline.

If you "did the math," you noticed we budgeted 189 minutes to complete this sample process—though probably some of that time is overlap, so the total will be closer to 180 minutes of actual work. If all goes well—and it should if you have practiced to meet the expected task speed—you should have plenty of time to succeed in the 195 minutes allotted.

Of course, this example is formulated only to help illustrate the practice premise. You will have to time yourself on each task in order to develop your own benchmark for the timeline to be constructed. This type of self-study is crucial, not only to your success on the certification practical, but to understanding your capabilities and applying them to your daily work regime. It will also give you a quantified basis from which you can begin to challenge yourself, to identify where those challenges lie.

Portion/score/marinate salmon, 10 minutes.
Break down lobsters/splint tails, 8 minutes.
Butcher chicken, prepare scalopini, season, 15 minutes.
Stack bacon and freeze for dicing later.
Put small, cut chicken bones to roast.
Prepare lobster stock, 12 minutes.
Start béchamel, 12 minutes.
Put artichokes to cook, 5 minutes.
Put bones in chicken stock with mirepoix to fortify for sauce, 8 minutes.
Pare fennel and put to braise, 8 minutes. *
Poach lobster tails in stock; remove; chill in a sealed plastic bag with small amount of stock, all in ice bath.
Prepare apple vinaigrette, 12 minutes.
Cut onions and soak in buttermilk, 5 minutes.
Prepare subric mixture, 10 minutes.
Marinate tomatoes, 5 minutes.
Put potatoes to cook for mash, 5 minutes.
Put milk to warm with butter/rosemary, for mash.
Pare carrots and put to glaze, 5 minutes. *
Add artichokes to subric mixture, 8 minutes.
Prepare sauce garnish, 8 minutes
Clean and slice lobster tail; prepare to reheat with butter and stock, 8 minutes.
Render bacon crisp; drain; keep warm, 2 minutes.
Flour and deep-fry onions; drain; keep warm, 4 minutes.
Put lemon chive sauce to finish/thicken, 8 minutes.
Finish mash; keep warm, 3 minutes.
Cut chives.
Clean and set for service, 10 minutes.
Finish lemon chive sauce, during setup.
Cook subrics during setup.
Begin service; be up with fish in 4 minutes.

Course 1
Sear fish.
Reheat tail.
Reheat fennel.
Sauce and chive garnish
Set all mise en place for main to warm.
Spinach cakes

*As item is finished, put into storage setup for quick reheat at service.

(continues)

Figure 3 Timeline for Exam Practice

Mash potatoes
Carrots
Sauce
Course 2, 6 minutes
Dress greens.
Plate salad.
Course 3, 8 minutes
Sautéed Chicken Breast Scaloppini
Build pan sauce.
Plating

Figure 3   Timeline for Exam Practice (Continued)

ADDRESSING THE SUBSETS OF THE COOKING PRACTICAL

Earlier in the book we introduced you to the ACF's foundational subsets (sanitation, basic skills, visual appeal, flavor and texture, etc.) with which a skilled cook at any level must become knowledgeable and skilled in order to become certified. In this chapter, we delve further into these subsets as each relates to the taking of the practical exam.

Sanitation

In modern kitchens, not surprisingly, sanitation and clean work habits are top priorities; thus it follows that to qualify to take the practical exam you will be expected to be certified in sanitation and be able to complete your tasks without violating any of the local sanitation codes.

Your workstation at the exam facility should be kept neat and clean at all times, and your performance should demonstrate that you understand why it is so important that cooks be concerned at every turn with this subject. This under-

UP TO CODE

It's important to point out that the sanitation section of the exam is a core competency and is graded as pass/fail. This means that if you fail this segment of the exam, you will be unsuccessful for the day.

standing also should be reflected in your appearance, the condition of your tools and all of your travel containers, and the way you store your gear once you have readied your station for the exam. Many candidates make the mistake, for example, of moving items from the floor onto a work surface, or stowing travel gear in an unsafe manner.

Pay close attention, as well, to the following sanitation issues, which are part and parcel of the operation of any kitchen or workstation:

- Time temperature violations
- Cross-contamination
- Proper dilution and use of all sanitizing agents (read labels carefully!)
- Correct "doneness" of *all* proteins, according to health codes
- Hand washing and glove use
- Ware washing
- Safety standards for the workplace

Basic Skills

Regardless of the level of certification for which you are applying, each carries with it a basic skill set that you will be expected to perform satisfactorily. And, as noted throughout the book, at each higher level that skill set is expanded. This applies to cooking methods and butchery, as well as the execution of knife cuts and fundamental product processes such as roux, beurre manié, and the variety of starches used to create various textures, flavor profiles, and visual attributes to any given sauce.

The methodology you apply to every aspect of your production will be evaluated and considered in your final score, so this is where and when your book study and practice will prove invaluable. Make the time before the exam, then, to refresh your memory by reviewing fundamentals-of-cooking reference books. No matter how knowledgeable and experienced you are, review is essential. As we've said so often, with increased industry experience comes greater expectation of deftness of execution and understanding of methodology, maturing to the point at which sound fundamental skills become second nature. Whatever your level of expertise, during the practical exam, you must be able to demonstrate the level-appropriate skills, in addition to the all-important fundamental skills.

Organization

A professional is expected to be able to work in an organized fashion to accomplish any assignment. The key factors to succeeding here are thorough planning, such as the timeline exercise described earlier, and, of course, practice!

The workflow and physical organization of your station are the primary areas of evaluation in this category—the storage of mise en place, the way you arrange your tools, how you manage your stovetop, your movement between tasks and handling of overlapping of tasks, and, finally, how you serve and present the program. Be conscious of all your movements and methods, whether you are managing small demonstration trays of cuts or storing vegetable by-products left from their manicuring for use in a three-course meal.

Utilization of Ingredients

You as a culinarian must understand the various parts of each food item you prepare. Each food has its parts: the primary and secondary cuts, the trim, and in most cases, the waste. All things in nature have their purpose, but when it comes to food, all cooks will discover that each has one particular purpose for which it is ideally suited.

It is the cook's greatest challenge to know what every edible substance "does" best. At the same time, the cook must work to learn how best to manicure, dismantle, or otherwise make the product ready for the cooking process. This involves making the correct and best use of all the secondary parts—which too many irresponsibly refer to as "garbage." Don't throw out usable by-products. For example, you can make bread from the inside of a zucchini; braise hearts of celery; use the insides of tomatoes (seeds removed) in sauces; incorporate chicken trimmings to add flavor to stock; use meat trimmings for stews; and add the outside of artichokes to make puree for delicious soup.

In this category of the exam, you will be evaluated on whether or not you understand how to take each food apart to provide the most sensible yield for its chosen use, as well as what to do with the parts that are not needed. Thus, for the exam, prepare food as if you were in your own kitchen: separate waste from trim that can be utilized at a later time; wrap it and store it as the useful item it still is. Don't fall prey to the thought that this is "just a test" and so fail to operate as you do every day. This is, perhaps, the single worst decision a candidate can make. Remember: work and produce food the same as you always do, exhibiting all the skills and methods that are part of your day-to-day routine. These exams are designed to discover flaws or errors in a cook's methodology, so don't make the mistake of trying to change your routine to disguise a lack of training, ability, or skill. The point is to find out whether you are ready to be certified and, if not, to learn what you need to do to become certified at a later date.

Flavor and Texture Development

To make food that tastes good: this is at the heart of all our years of work, the countless dollars spent on our education, and the effort of absorbing knowledge from our mentors. It is curious, then, that this basic premise is often overlooked or undervalued by those taking the practical exam. Many chefs simply never take the time to evaluate for themselves whether what they have prepared is enjoyable. Veteran chefs in particular, after many years of toil in the kitchen, sometimes become jaded; to them food becomes a "manufacturing material." Yes, they may follow the proper preparation methodology, and produce attractive, safe food, but they don't think to dine, from time to time, on their own cuisine. This can happen—and does, all too often—to chefs in any environment, whether a hospital, school, or high-volume, high-class restaurant.

The best way to avoid this pitfall is to devote enough time to sample the flavor, taste, and texture of the foods you prepare—

as well as that of other foodservice establishments. In addition, it's a good idea to make an ongoing study of how to impart good flavor and textural attributes to all your dishes, always with your clientele and your own professional development in mind. Even if your menu does not change often, it behooves you to continually perform due diligence where the quality of flavor and texture are concerned.

In terms of the certification exam, plan to develop simple, delicious flavor profiles that you can generate in a less than laborious fashion, primarily through sound methodology and good seasoning. This, of course, applies to pastry as well, particularly when it comes to the amount of sweetness and the use of liquor or the many flavoring agents available to the pastry chef. Relate the flavors and textures from one dish or plate component to another, so that they compose a harmonious whole. A word of warning is in order here: this exam is not the time to experiment; err on the side of caution, favoring conservative flavor combinations. Don't forget, though creativity is certainly appreciated, it does not have any bearing on your score during a practical exam.

When it comes to texture, plan to build variety into the dishes. At the same time, it is important to examine the grouping of textures on the plate to confirm they work with one another and complement the flavors being used. Think of the pleasure of eating a simple vegetable soup: flavor aside, the textures of this fundamental dish can make it very unpleasant or pleasurable, depending on the "bite" associated with the vegetable garnish. If the vegetables are overcooked and have no consistency, you will be denied the pleasure of biting through a perfectly cooked piece of celery as the hot liquid swirls in your mouth. Or consider the pleasing "pop" of a perfectly cooked piece of barley, coupled with the smooth, soft bite of a mushroom slice in a perfectly prepared mushroom and barley pilaf; or how wonderful the contrast between the ideal crispness of pâte à choux and the smooth chocolate and the fluffy cream filling, which make an éclair the taste treat it is. These sensations seriously impact the pleasure derived by the diner, thus you need to make food texture an important aspect of your cooking skills—certainly as you prepare for the practical exam.

97

FOR THE INTERMEDIATE CULINARIAN

At this stage of your career, you should be focusing more of your study and research on what exactly is "good taste"; in other words, what makes the flavor of a dish perceived as pleasant, enjoyable, or "good." This is an elusive concept (after all, what tastes good to one person might not to another) to master, and so is an extensive undertaking, requiring a great deal of experience and effort. At the intermediate level, you should have a basic understanding of what is tasteful and saleable to the clientele, most of which comes from your knowledge of basic cooking methodology and seasoning. You also need to learn how to execute the cooking methods to enhance, or at least retain, the natural textures you have decided to use in your dish.

At your experience level, it will be assumed that you have an understanding of the importance of taste and texture, so during your exam you will be asked to create some fundamental items, all meant to examine your ability to execute cooking fundamentals and basic culinary products, such as mother sauces or vegetable preparations. On the CCC/CWPC exam, you will be challenged to formulate dishes in conjunction with the mise en place components.

Practice at this level is essential, along with as much feedback as possible from mentors, particularly in the area of taste texture and flavor.

Craftsmanship

All chefs are expected to be craftsmen—how deftly we cut a vegetable; smoothly remove the flesh from a fish; peel, in a single motion, a shrimp; perfectly slice a cooked roast. Perhaps in no other area of the exam will practice and repetition "tell the tale." Simply put, if you don't practice, you will not be able to perform at the top of your form—as a craftsman.

For the purpose of certification, to achieve craftsmanship,

PRACTICE MAKES CRAFT

There is a fine line between craftsmanship and technical expertise—the correct execution of fundamental cooking processes. Craftsmanship refers to the more subtle well-practiced skills that a chef develops over time. Craftsmanship can be seen in the smooth and quick butchery of a whole pig, the deft icing of a torte, or the careful peeling of a carrot. Seemingly effortless, in fact it is time, practice, and, most of all, interest in the subtleties of the craft that define the difference between a great craftsman and a technician. That said, there is plenty of room for both in our industry.

take the time to understand all the detailed aspects of process execution, in particular the knife skills. It will be important to be able to produce a well-crafted cut, such as a julienne or tourné, and to know which product and cooking method it is best utilized for.

Visual Appeal

Simplicity is the guiding principle here. Remember that everyone "eats with their eyes" first. Imagine, for example, a cook who lays a chicken breast next to a bundle of green beans, neatly drizzles a sauce on half of the breast and part of the plate, then tumbles three nicely browned, tournéed potatoes into a group, and finishes by adding a bit of caramelized mushrooms and shallots. Visual appeal is the "quiet skill"; it reflects a cook's ability to place food on a plate in an appetizing fashion.

Becoming proficient in this competency, as all others required by the practical exam, takes practice and planning. To be able to lay pastries on a platter in such a way that blends curved lines and straight, a chef must develop an artistic "eye," for the skill in visual composition. It is a skill that necessitates an understanding of how shapes, colors, lines, and negative space all work together to create a visually pleasing grouping. But it is more, for when the artistic "medium" is food, the chef must also consider serviceability of the food, for if it is presented in such a way that makes it difficult to eat, then the cook has failed.

To explore this subject with zeal, you should take a class in visual composition; but, in general, it is not necessary to go to this length to succeed at the cooking practical at any level. More applicable here is to seek the advice of your mentors and rely on your culinary training. For the purpose of the exam, plating need only be neat, attractive, sensible to serve, and maintain the integrity of all items on the plate. Here, too, as discussed in the previous section, consider the textures that have been developed either through methodology or preparation type. In other words, do not place a crisp item in a sauce, thereby softening its crunch. Along this line of thought, don't forget to correctly blot items to avoid liquids leaching into sauces and rendering them watery or damaging their color.

Nutritional Understanding

As cooks, it is our basic responsibility to nourish our patrons, so we need a comprehensive knowledge of nutrients and how they affect the human body; we need to know the good and bad of anything we intend to feed someone. That is why, at every level of certification, there is a nutritional education requirement.

A COOK'S RESPONSIBILITY

A responsibility to nourish our patrons does not imply that we should cook in a low-calorie or other trendy style, or that we should try and direct our customers to what they "should" eat.

When it comes to meeting the nutritional cooking requirement for the practical exam, perhaps the best advice is to begin by using the freshest, prime ingredients you can obtain; and do your shopping as close to exam time as possible. Do not just grab a tomato; select the best-looking tomato you can find. Do not use a frozen steak; purchase a choice strip loin, and cut the best piece for the exam. Do not buy the lower-quality apricot nappage; use the best one.

In the planning stages, you will need to consider the balance, of the dish or meal and be able to demonstrate your knowledge of how that balance should be represented in a single dish or within a meal, whichever the case. Next address the seasoning: first use the herbs, spices, vinegars, and delicious stocks to impart flavor; then move to the fats and salt to finish. Finally, move to the execution of cooking methods; this is where you enhance the natural flavors of the products through good cooking. If a sauce is part of your requirements, and you are simply preparing a mother sauce or other basic mise en place product, you will rely totally on the execution of the method, including the measurement of fats to be used and quality of ingredients, as no seasoning is required until that product is used later.

No matter what you are preparing, being conscious of nutrition means you consider carefully what you are feeding to people—what that food consists of. Generally speaking, it will mean proper balance and correct cooking techniques, with the food minimally enhanced with added fat and salt.

CONCLUSION

As a cook or chef, it is your responsibility to feed people in any circumstance, and by passing the ACF practical exam, you and the American Culinary Federation are assuring the public that you are qualified to do so; you are a certified chef or culinarian, a true professional.

The practical testing process is constructed to comprehensively evaluate your skills, and is not meant to be simple, so you must take the proper steps to prepare yourself if you are to be successful. Plan and practice: those are the two best pieces of advice we can give you.

FREQUENTLY ASKED QUESTIONS ABOUT THE PRACTICAL EXAM

How many times should I practice?
For the full-timed scenario, at least 10. Begin by practicing the exam in its individual parts, developing your timeline and then putting it together. This will be a faster process for some than for others. But speed is not the issue, if this was a simple process it would never get the respect it is meant to, nor would the certification garnered be as meaningful.

What happens if I am late on my time frame?

The short answer is that, in most cases, it will result in a point loss to some extent. The number of points will depend on:

- The reason for the lateness
- Your understanding of why you were late, in conjunction with your ability to recover
- Whether you were able to notify the evaluators of your need to present late and then follow the timing mandated by the evaluators

Whatever the reason, in all cases notify the evaluation staff of your problem and be prepared to accept the evaluator's determination. Your food will be rescheduled for a different presentation time, which of course might affect the quality of the food, but that is the price you will pay for untimely production. In some cases, excessive lateness can cause failure. This call will be made by the evaluators, who will inform you of their decision.

What should I do if my food has been damaged in transit?

Inform the test administrator of the problem; he or she will do everything possible to help resolve the situation. If, however, the food cannot be suitably replaced, the exam may need to be postponed.

Who is responsible for the correct titration of my sanitizing solution?

You are. Although many systems are automatic and should be correct, they are not always. Ultimately, the responsibility for all sanitation requirements falls on you, the candidate.

Is a helper or apprentice allowed?

No; the only helper will be a dishwasher or equivalent, who should be provided by the exam site. And, note, you may be assessed a charge for this service.

Must I prepare classical items?

Only if you use classical terminology in your menu—with the exception of matignon vegetable and the consommé garnish, which is derived from a classical garnish, meaning you will use

Escoffier as a source. No level other than CMC/CMPC requires the preparation of classical dishes.

Must I prepare a printed menu?

Yes, you must prepare a list of items you will produce during the exam, and it is those items you must present for evaluation. If the level requires a menu, it should be presented for the evaluators to view during your production. And it should be professionally presented, as it will be part of your evaluation.

Do I need printed recipes?

Recipes are suggested for many of the processes to be evaluated; however, they are for your own support system. The recipe itself will not be evaluated, only the product derived from the recipe.

What is a fish course?

A fish course is a preliminary course during a meal and should be constructed as an appetizer. The portion should be that of a starter course; the balance and flavor profile should be considered as part of the entire meal presented, the same as any course in a single dining experience.

May I cross-utilize products during the pastry exam?

Yes, as long as each cross-utilization is used as a supporting ingredient or mise en place. In other words, it would not be acceptable to present a torte filled with vanilla Bavarian cream and a plated dessert built around a timbale of vanilla Bavarian cream, whereas it would be acceptable to have that same torte and then build the dessert around a raspberry Bavarian.

Is there any substitute for the practical test?

Very few activities can substitute for the practical exam at the CEC level and below, and there is no approved substitution for the CMC exam. The following are acceptable replacements: membership on Team USA or the ACF National Culinary Olympic Team, or a silver medal or above in category F/1 or F/5.

Who are the best people to help me prepare for my exam?
ACF judges, experienced exam evaluators, CMCs/CMPCs, chefs who have taken and passed the exam at the same level, and seasoned competitors.

I am not a competitive person. Can I still succeed?
Absolutely! Even though the formats and evaluation criteria of the practical exams resemble a competition, there really is no correlation. The only true similarity is that both are based on cooking fundamentals.

To whom should I direct questions?
The ACF welcomes all questions regarding the practical testing process. It is our mission to make the process as user-friendly as possible. All candidates are encouraged to explore all available avenues to gather the information they need so that their testing day runs smoothly. For questions regarding exam requirements, contact the ACF Certification Chair; regarding paperwork, the ACF National Office; regarding the actual test or facility, the test administrator.

The Application Process

WHEN YOU FEEL READY TO APPLY FOR ACF CERTIFICATION, the manner in which you compile the required information, collect and attach the validating documents, and submit all the final paperwork will either aid or hamper the successful completion of the process. Everything in the application packet is minutely scrutinized and verified, so the easier it is to do that, the faster you will receive positive results, along with the signed certification certificate and wallet card.

To the reviewers charged with validating the skills and knowledge represented on an application, completeness, accuracy, and neatness of the application packet are critical. Dated information, blanks, or even errors on the forms can jeopardize the review process and delay your getting the certification recognition you deserve. What normally can take a few days to validate can take as long as three to four months to process because of incorrect or insufficient information.

APPLICATION BASICS

Applications for ACF certifications can take three different forms: initial certifications, renewal certifications, and upgraded certifications. Each type requires different sets of information and documentation, while still concentrating on education and skill development. Here is a description of each form and the type of information they require:

> **Initial certifications.** Cooks and chefs are applying for ACF certification at any level for the first time. These candidates must document all education, experience, and tests required for the level of certification they are seeking.
>
> **Renewal certifications.** Cooks and chefs are fulfilling the five-year renewal requirement for all ACF-certified cooks and chefs when staying at the same certification level. They must submit documentation of mandatory course refreshers (minimum of eight hours each), plus continuing education hours required by the level of certification from approved sources.
>
> **Upgraded certifications.** Culinarians applying for upgraded certifications have garnered the additional education and experience required for a higher level of certification than they currently hold. The ACF maintains the original records of all active certified cooks and chefs, and uses these files as reference for the original levels of education and experience; thus, certification candidates who are upgrading only need to document the additional information necessary for the higher level of certification, along with the mandatory refresher courses if older than five years.

Before you fill out an application and/or submit the forms to ACF's office for review, you should have fulfilled all the necessary requirements and obtained all the appropriate paperwork required for the level of certification you are seeking. Only complete applications will be processed. Incomplete applications will be returned to you minus a small administrative fee for handling.

Some basic guidelines to follow when collecting evidence of

skill and knowledge proficiencies and submitting the paper-work for your certification applications include the following:

1. Be accurate and neat when filling out your application. Type or print all information carefully.
2. Submit only the paperwork asked for in the application. Additional materials, such as press releases, resumes, newspaper articles, and/or letters of reference (unless such letters validate employment), are not needed.
3. Accompany all information on the application with appropriate documentation, which may include photo-copies of diplomas, transcripts, certificates, and letters verifying educational activities. Where original docu-mentation is not available for photocopying, sworn, notarized statements may be accepted.
4. Do not send any original documents unless specified, as these will not be filed in the office nor returned to you.
5. Accompany all documents that are written in a language other than English with a notarized English translation. Translations of foreign educational degrees and appren-ticeship programs should state the type of degree or apprenticeship, its American equivalent where appropri-ate, the list of subjects/courses covered, and the amount of hours of education each one represents.
6. Do not use outside covers, plastic page covers, binders or any other type of document organizer/holder. In order to place the approved application and its contents in ACF's permanent files, all of these items must be removed. Simply insert all the required documentation, along with the application and fees, in a large envelope and mail it to ACF National Office, 180 Center Place Way, St. Augus-tine, Florida 32095.
7. In most cases, include only one piece of documentation for each entry. Only one copy of the school or college transcript is needed to verify compliance to the manda-tory course requirement, even if multiple courses are represented on the single form.
8. Don't send the work verification forms if you have a letter on company letterhead detailing the beginning/ ending dates of employment, job title, and a brief expla-

nation of duties. Don't forget to include current phone number and contact information, as this is critical to verifying experience.

9. Do not include résumés to validate experience or education, as they are *not* considered official work documentation.

When assembling the application, organize and label the material in the manner described in the following sections. Either mark the top, right-hand corner of each corresponding document with the appropriate insignia, or use tabbed inserts with the appropriate marks written on them, as identified in the section titles below.

Mandatory Requirements

The mandatory requirements are numbered M-1 to M-8 and are defined as follows:

M-1 Written Exam Verification—Letter from the ACF or an official ACF testing center showing a score of 70 percent or higher on the level-specific written exam

M-2 Practical Certification Exam—Letter from the ACF or official practical test site showing a score of 70 percent or higher on the level-specific cooking and/or baking exam

M-3 Other Practical Proficiency—If substituting for practical test, letter or official document from authorized testing agency or culinary committee

M-4 400-plus/minus-Word Essay (Certified Culinary Administrator only)—Typed or handwritten narrative outlining your daily tasks and responsibilities as defined by your position as culinary administrator

M-5 30-Hour Nutrition Course*—Transcripts, certificates, or letters of successful completion from approved sources

*Requires eight-hour refresher every five years

M-6 30-Hour Sanitation and Food Safety Course*—Transcripts, certificates, or letters of successful completion from approved sources

M-7 30-Hour Supervision and Management Course*—Transcripts, certificates, or letters of successful completion from approved sources

M-8 30-Hour Personal Chef Course (Personal Chef levels only)—Transcripts, certificates, or letters of successful completion from approved sources

In addition, you will need documentation of successful completion for an additional 8 hours of education in the same subject area from an approved source, if the 30-hour course is older than five years; on initial applications, both the mandatory 30-hour course and 8-hour refresher courses must be documented in the application if the original 30-hour course is older than five years.

Formal Education

Here is the information you need to complete the formal education category of the certification application:

- You will need to document diplomas, certificates, and degrees, either with school transcripts (transcripts are required for the mandatory courses) or with copies of the actual certificates or diplomas, which must display the school's name and/or seal and must clearly display the date and appropriate signatures. Note: *Do not send originals of these materials.*
- Formal education, as documented in the form of diplomas, certificates, or degrees, does not have to be based on culinary or foodservice subjects to earn educational credit. The diplomas and degrees represent academic value, which the ACF recognizes is needed for professional success.
- All "other education" (in addition to formal diplomas, certificates, or degrees) and continuing education courses

---

*Requires eight-hour refresher every five years

must be related to foodservice, hospitality, or business subjects.

When applying for ACF certification, you need to document only the highest academic degree you earned, as you will receive credit for only one degree, diploma, or certificate.

The following list specifies how the section on academic achievement is shown on the ACF certification application. You will choose the highest degree you've earned, back it up with appropriate documentation, and claim the accompanying educational point values (which are listed on the latest application, or ACF Web site) leading toward your professional certification.

E-7.1 **High School diploma/GED**—Copy of diploma or school transcript, showing date of completion

E-7.2 **Certified Graduate from an ACF Secondary Accredited Program**—Copy of diploma or school transcript, showing date of completion

E-7.3 **Postsecondary Diploma/Certificate or Nondegree Apprenticeship Program**—Copy of diploma, certificate, school transcript, or apprentice graduation certificate, showing date of completion

E-7.4 **ACF Apprenticeship Degree Program (three years)**—Copy of certificate, showing date of completion

E-7.5 **Associate's Degree**—Copy of degree certificate or transcript, showing date of completion

E-7.6 **Bachelor's Degree**—Copy of degree certificate or transcript, showing date of completion

E-7.7 **Master's Degree**—Copy of degree certificate or transcript, showing date of completion

E-7.8 **Doctorate (earned degrees only)**—Copy of degree certificate or transcript, showing date of completion

Other Education

In addition to documenting formal academic education, you are permitted to submit evidence of other forms of education in order to earn additional education credit. But in order to qualify for certification credits, these nondiploma/certificate programs must be related to the foodservice or hospitality industry, in production, service, business, or management.

The following list contains useful information pertaining to submitting informal educational experiences for consideration:

E-1 THROUGH E-7 (AS NEEDED)

- Education credit is given for any approved course(s) related to the foodservice and hospitality industry.
- Candidates earn one education credit for every six hours of instruction they take.
- Acceptable documentation includes copies of certificates or official letters of attendance, listing the subject name and hours and dates of attendance.
- Education credit may also be awarded to successful medalists in ACF- and WACS-sanctioned culinary competitions (bronze, silver, and gold medal entries qualify for education credit).

Professional Work Experience/Employment Verifications

Before filling out the application itself it is a good idea to list all your job experiences on a separate piece of paper (both part-time and full-time); as part of this list, be sure to include job titles, duties, and the beginning and end dates of your employment (month, day, and year wherever possible). Arrange this information in chronological order (starting with your first job and ending with your current or most recent position), and attach the appropriate documentation to your application.

In addition, follow these other guidelines for documenting your professional experience:

- Be able to account for all of the experience required for the level of certification for which you are applying.
- Document only those experiences required for your level of certification. And, note, you do not have to include evidence that is older than 10 years, *unless* it is needed to justify the level of certification being sought.

- Claim only one job for any specific time period, even if you worked more than one full-time job in the same time period.
- Generally, you can only earn experience points for full-time jobs that you held continuously for at least one year (except for CC, CPC, and seasonal employment). Any position that was not full-time or ended before 12 months of continuous service was completed may not be counted. There are, however, two exceptions where less than a full year of experience may be counted:
- Part-time experience while attending school or college may be counted for CC and CPC levels of certification; 2,080 hours of work experience equates to one year of full-time work.
- Documented seasonal employment where the operation is open only for specific periods during the year due to climate or seasonality; experience may be counted on a month-to-month basis (one month earns 0.5 point credit; six months earns 3 experience points, etc.). You are rewarded for staying at the same establishment for more than one year (12 months) and for each consecutive year afterward by earning a greater number of experience points based on the longevity of each position held.

If you work for the same company for multiple years but in different locations (for example, in a corporate hotel chain or corporate foodservice management company), you earn experience points as if you had worked in a single location.

Work experience points for ACF certification are based on the schedule in Table 1. An additional 0.5 point of experience is

TABLE 1   Work Experience Points Based on Length of Employment at Each Company/Position

Full Year at Same Company or Position	Experience Points (Noncumulative)
First year	6 points
Second year	13 points
Third year	21 points
Fourth year*	30 points

*Add 10 points per year after the initial four years in any given job

awarded for every month worked after each 12 months at the same operation or with the same company. For example, say you worked one year and one month in the same position: you would earn 6 points for the first year and 0.5 point for the additional month worked, for a total of 6.5 points; one year and two months would equal a total of 7 points. And if you worked for the same company for two and a half years (30 months), you would earn 13 points for the first two years and 3 additional points for the other six months worked, for a total of 19 experience points. These points are posted on the certification application adjacent to the cited work experience and followed by a labeled (W-1 through W-6) verification document.

You must document all work experience with either the official form (ACF Certification Employment Documentation Form), included with the official application, or a formal letter on company letterhead containing all the required information (i.e., person's name, place of employment, dates of employment, duties/responsibilities while employed, and number of people supervised). Also, you must attach labels for work verifications to each citation (W–1 through W–6), in order from earliest position to the most recent.

Level-Specific Experience

It is important to remember that the purpose of the ACF certification process is to validate the skills and knowledge of culinarians, helping them to be successful in the positions they seek or already hold; ACF certification is *not* a license to practice the craft at those levels. Therefore, each candidate must document his or her successful experience (employment in a position of 12 months or longer) at the respective level of certification, in addition to any prerequisite experience required for each level.

For example, culinarians applying for Certified Culinarian or Pastry Culinarian only need to document experience at the cook's or pastry cook's level, whereas candidates for Sous Chef/Working Pastry Chef certification must be able to document two years work experience at that level, in addition to three or more years of general cooking/baking experience. As you know by now, each level of certification has a different

ACF ADHERENCE TO THE ADA

The ACF supports the intent of the Americans with Disabilities Act (ADA), and to that end makes every possible allowance to ensure that every certification candidate with a disability can complete the application process. As this applies to the practical and written examinations, the ACF offers only auxiliary aids and services that do not fundamentally alter how skills or knowledge are measured during the exams [see Americans with Disabilities Act, Public Law 101-334 §309(b)(3)]. For more information on, or to learn how to make arrangements for, special accommodations for either the written or practical exam requirements, please notify the ACF National Office's certification coordinator or director of education by calling 800-624-9458 or by writing to the ACF Education Office at 180 Center Place Way, St. Augustine, Florida 32095.

requirement for level-specific versus general experience. These requirements are updated on the current ACF certification application, which is available from the ACF National Office or the Web site (www.acfchefs.org).

COMPLETING THE APPLICATION PROCESS

Once you have collected all of your records, including proof of completion of required skills or knowledge competency tests, and made copies of all pertinent documents, transcripts, and/ or letters verifying work history, you are ready to complete your application process. The steps you take at this juncture will determine how fast your application will be reviewed and the information it contains verified, for either accepting or denying your certification request. As stated at the beginning of the chapter, incomplete, unclear, and inaccurate applications will hamper the review process, causing extended delays in processing, which could result in the rejection and return of your application.

To help you in this all-important endeavor, we conclude this chapter with a checklist of important to-do's for filling out your application:

1. Either type or print clearly and neatly.
2. Supply all the information specified on the application, except where noted as "Optional." Optional information is gathered to help the ACF develop demographic profiles for certified cooks and chefs; you do not have to fill out these areas, nor will it jeopardize your certification in any way if you choose not to.
3. Provide your full contact information: address, phone number(s), and e-mail address. Your personal contact information is vital to the process, in case the ACF office staff needs to get in touch with you regarding a question on your application.
4. Choose the level of certification you are applying for, and mark your application appropriately.
5. Check the ACF Web site or call its national office to get the latest fee schedule for ACF certifications; include payment with your application.
6. Read, sign, and date the Certification Agreement statement on your application. This grants to ACF officers and staff dealing with certifications the rights to investigate your statements and documents for their authenticity and accuracy through whatever means they have at their disposal. This information will be used only for the determination of certification, and will be kept confidential in ACF certification files. Without your signature consenting to the ACF's investigative rights pursuant to the certification application process, your application cannot be processed and will be returned to you.
7. Check "Yes" or "No" to the question giving the ACF rights to advertise or otherwise promote your certification, should it be granted, in local newspapers, national magazines, and/or on the ACF Web site. Selecting "Yes" will allow the ACF to promote your accomplishments and those of the operation you work for, along with the benefits of ACF's certification program to employers and consumers. Selecting "No" will not interfere with the due processing of your application and will preclude the ACF advertising or promoting your certification achievements in any way.

115

8. Label all corresponding verification documents in the top right-hand corner to coincide with the matrix on the application, as follows:

   a. M-1 through M-8 to denote satisfactory completion of the mandatory requirements

   b. E-7.1 through E-7.8 for earned diplomas, certificates, apprenticeships, or degrees

   c. E-1 through E-7 (as needed) to document additional education

   d. W-1 through W-6 (as needed) to document working experience in chronological order, beginning with earliest position held, along with position titles, dates (in the form, MM/DD/YYYY), and their corresponding point values based on the experience charts given here and on the application itself

9. Make as many copies of the ACF Certification Employment Documentation Form as needed and fill one out for each job/position held. Each form must contain the current address and phone number(s) for each place of employment, along with the signature of the supervisor or manager authenticating the information.

10. Add up the points in each category, then verify that you have met the point requirements for the certification level you are applying for. [Culinary educators, secondary educators, personal chefs, and culinary administrators each have slightly different certification requirements pursuant to their areas of expertise. These requirements can be found on the ACF Web site (www.acfchefs.org) or can be obtained by calling the ACF national office.]

11. Double-check all entries and documents to ensure you have completed the application properly; place all documents in a single large envelope (do not fold the documents).

12. Send completed application with fees to:

    ACF Education Department

    180 Center Place Way

    St. Augustine, Florida 32095

ACF APPLICATION FREQUENTLY ASKED QUESTIONS

What qualifies for the mandatory courses in Sanitation, Supervision, and Nutrition?

Any college-level course (2 college credits) on the subjects qualifies when offered by an accredited institution. The requirement is for 30 classroom hours in each subject area, which may include time for testing. Some programs may substitute outside reading assignments or research projects for some of the required hours, provided there is a formal assessment of the work completed. In all cases, classroom time should be at least 50 percent of the total required hours. Call the ACF Education Department for a current course syllabus for each area to compare required competencies with existing programs.

Must a school have ACF accreditation to qualify for education programming?

No. Schools and colleges must be accredited by either the state or regional accreditation agency in the area in which they operate, but not by the ACF's Accrediting Commission, which offers programmatic accreditation only to culinary schools and programs.

Where can I find the three mandatory courses offered?

Most often, cooks and chefs take these courses in the military, as part of their college degree, or during an apprenticeship program. The ACF also approves hospitality programs (e.g., NRA and AHM&LA), educational institution courses (e.g., community colleges or vocational-technical schools), and chapter-sponsored programs, when the mandatory courses are offered in a venue suited to the candidates. Already approved programs can be found on the ACF Web page under Professional Development and/or Certification.

When do I need a refresher course in the three mandatory areas?

You will need to take a refresher for each area if your coursework is five years or older. Throughout your career you will need to take a refresher course for each subject every five years.

What qualifies for an eight-hour refresher course?
Many refresher courses are offered on a one-day (eight-hour)
classroom schedule by accredited schools and colleges, ACF
chapters, and during ACF conferences and conventions.
Refresher courses must feature the most up-to-date information
available for the given subject. You may take a course from any
ACF preapproved provider, such as www.chefcertification.com
for online learning, or the American Academy of Independent
Studies (AAIS), www.123ce.com, for correspondence (through
the mail) courses.

How do I count educational degrees?
Select the highest earned degree from among the list provided in
this chapter (E- 7.1 – E 7.8) and on the application itself. Count
only the points associated with the highest degree earned, no
matter how many additional degrees you have. For example,
even if you have two master's degrees, you may only count one
of them, for a total of 35 points (not 70 points). Likewise, though
you would have earned master's and bachelor's degrees in
addition to any earned doctorate, only points awarded for the
doctorate may be counted (40 points) for certification.

What is the ACF looking for in the work experience area?
The ACF requires documentation of level-specific work experience and additional work experience in all but the first level of
certification. Work experience must be cooking/baking in
nature for all cook and chef levels of certifications. Carefully
read the job description for the level you are applying for.
Describe and document the specific work experience for that
level, plus all additional work experience needed to total the
amount required. If you do not have the minimum number of
points in the specific category, you should consider applying for
the next certification level down.

How do I document work experience if I am self-employed?
Submit copies of a business license or tax documents (not
the tax return, just the portion that verifies that you own the

business). You can also include letters from your business accountant or attorney to verify ownership.

What should I do if an operation I worked for has gone out of business?

First, determine whether you need the points from that employment to acquire the level of certification you are seeking. Most culinarians applying for a higher level of certification have more years of experience than are required for those levels. The ACF only needs to verify the amount of experience required, and nothing else. If you do need the points, make every effort to contact a former boss, supervisor, or company official who could verify your employment (position and dates) at the now-defunct business. Testimonials from supervisors, human resources directors, chefs, and even peers will be considered when all other avenues for work verification have been explored. Remember, though, the best advice is to collect documentation of your professional development as you move along in your career. At a minimum, make it a practice wherever you work to ask your supervisor(s) to write you a letter (on company letterhead) verifying your job title, duties/responsibilities, how many people you supervised, and dates of employment for each position. Do this even if you are not applying for ACF certification, as you may need these documents at a later date.

Should I send the ACF original documents?

In general, no; send copies of all other documents, including letters of recommendation, certificates, and diplomas. Only send originals when requested to do so, such as signed employment verification records.

How long is my certification package kept on file?

ACF keeps your application and package on file as long as your certification remains current. This makes it possible to research your package whenever you apply for a change in certification status. If and when a certified cook's or chef's certification lapses, his or her files are purged after a two-year grace period. It's a good idea to keep a copy of your package as well, to maintain an accurate and consistent record of what you have submitted previously, in case you need to reproduce it later.

Achieving the Ultimate Goal: Certified Master Chef

THE WORD TO WHICH YOU SHOULD HOLD FAST when thinking about becoming a Certified Master Chef (CMC) is "master." This prestigious title is earned by demonstrating a mastery of all the skills that make up the consummate chef—all things cooking, baking, or pastry, depending on which area one decides to master, as well as mentoring, sanitation, nutrition, and organization. When someone has "mastered" the skills of cookery or pastry, he or she has demonstrated an indisputably high level of competency in each area under evaluation.

At present, the Master Chef exam comprises an eight-day-long series of various tests devised to challenge the candidate to demonstrate his or her skills in a number of scenarios and cooking styles. Currently, the exam encompasses the following:

- Day 1—Healthy cooking
- Day 2/3—Buffet catering
- Day 4—Classical cuisine

- Day 5—Freestyle cooking
- Day 6—Global cuisine
- Day 7—Baking and pastry
- Day 8, a.m.—(the last day) European continent
- Day 8, p.m.—Mystery basket

Or for the certified master pastry chef a 10-day exam that comprises:

Dietary and Nutritional Baking
Baking Skills
Pastry Skills (Cakes and Tortes)
Baking Science
International Baking
Pastry Skills (Individual Desserts)
Food Service and Bakery Management
Pastry Grand Buffet

This lineup and the testing format have been revised many times over the more than 23-year history of the exam. The changing nature of the industry makes it necessary for the ACF to regularly reevaluate the testing process to ensure that it reflects current practices, at the same time maintaining the basic structure and outcome of the exam. It is easy to see from the curricula that the exam covers most facets of mainstream cooking and pastry production, while relying strongly on the foundational aspects of our craft.

If you are thinking of taking either exam, the first step in preparation is to self-evaluate your ability to execute each segment of the exam at the prescribed score of 70 percent or better (you must pass the whole with a score of 75 percent). Though you may repeat an individual segment, doing so is generally regarded as highly stressful, and so to be avoided at all costs. Better to be ready to pass all segments in a continuum. For the chefs the "last day," as it has become known, is a highly intense segment designed to compel the candidate to exhibit skills that should, at this level of proficiency, be second nature; it is marked by the large amount of work and the quick pace. For the Pastry chefs it is actually a three-day lab in which the pastry buffet is completed, but it is nearly impossible for any candidate to perform at an acceptable level unless he or she truly is a master of cooking or pastry arts.

DETAILS OF THE CMC TEST

The CMC program was initiated in 1981. The driving force behind it was Ferdinand Metz, CMC, AAC, founder and chairman of the Certified Master Chef Committee at that time. The Certified Master Chef or Pastry Chef level is the highest and most demanding level of achievement of all the certification levels, granted only after the candidate has passed the aforementioned intensive test of culinary skills and knowledge.

In October 1981, the first five ACF chefs qualified as CMCs: Byron Bardy, Milos Cihelka, Anton Flory, Dieter Kiessling, and Richard Schneider. (As of December 2004, there were 59 Certified Master Chefs and 12 Certified Master Pastry Chefs.) In 1982, the program was presented to the World Association of Cooks Societies (WACS) Congress in Vienna, Austria, and granted official recognition by that body. The Master Chef test is held annually—providing a minimum of six candidates have registered—and is judged by a panel of Certified Master Chefs and Certified Master Pastry Chefs. Presently, there are two approved test sites: the Culinary Institute of America (CIA) in Hyde Park, New York, and Greystone, the CIA's West Coast campus in Napa Valley, California.

Achieving CMC/CMPC should be a goal which is set early on in your career, for the skills you will need to pass the test are best developed along the way. With this exam as a goal, you will be challenging yourself for much of your career, whether it be in competition or just in the day-to-day expression of the skills needed to produce edible items to standard. In the process, you will come to understand food and its preparation better than you ever thought possible. You will also form valuable relationships while working to understand our craft at this level. Many of the people who help you along the way may become lifelong friends and mentors whose friendship, knowledge, and support will be important to your success.

It is much more difficult to learn to cook, work through 10

or 12 years of a career, and then decide to attempt the CMC exam, as many of the things that are expected ideally will have been nurtured as your skills matured. Very often it is far too obvious to evaluators when a candidate is trying to meet the demands of the exam, as opposed to exhibiting the well-honed skills he or she uses every day. Certainly talent plays a role, but there is no replacement for study, well-thought-out organization, and practice when it comes to taking this test. And, as discussed throughout this book, and particularly at the CMC level, it is important to seek out mentors (ideally, those who have achieved CMC status themselves) to critique you and share their knowledge. Of course, there are many chefs in our industry who possess mastery of certain elements of the exam, or who are qualified and simply are not interested in becoming a CMC, but, as the saying goes, "if you want to learn to milk a cow, go to the dairy farmer."

The CMC exam evaluators essentially judge everything a candidate does from the time he or she enters the test site until he or she leaves. Doing so sets a tone of professionalism and excellence. Thus, candidates should come prepared, with a solid understanding of what the exam is about and how it is run; it's also a good idea to be familiar with the exam site and the test administrator. It is up to you to cultivate the relationship which will ultimately benefit your success.

In answer to the common question, "How do I become a CMC," it is not overstating to say that everything you do in your career will play a part. It is stating the obvious to say that you must have a love of food and cooking, as well as a drive to become a master. More specifically, though, for the chefs mastery of the following subjects is essential: charcuterie, classical cookery, and the cookery of the European continent. For the Pastry Chefs, the same type of widescope knowledge relating to pastry arts is mandatory. That said, these are also the subjects that, for a variety of reasons, are not always commonly taught or practiced in this country's food industry. Nevertheless, they are the subjects that are eminently important to the fundamental understanding of cuisine and cooking—and to the professional development of a CMC or CMPC, a chef who has a tremendous breadth and depth of food knowledge, the culinary practices of the world, and the methodologies behind producing those cuisines. Therefore, it should be the mission of any CMC candidate to become intimately familiar with each of those areas and to master the techniques associated with them. The fact that it may be difficult to get a great deal of solid experience in these areas in the United States must be seen as just part of the challenge of accomplishing this meaningful goal.

CMC candidates should also be aware that, during the exam, they will be presented with a large variety of foods and will be required to have mastered the techniques necessary to make those groceries what they should be. Likewise, the pastry chefs will be challenged with virtually every type of baking and pastry preparation known. The best way to meet this challenge is to make an inventory of each and every food product that would be reasonably expected to appear and begin to study as many of those grocery items or methods as you can acquire beforehand. All the while, keep records and develop a repertoire for your intended project. The objective here is twofold: first, to increase your knowledge and understanding so that your skills improve to the point of mastery; and, second, to create a plan of action for any given circumstance, so that when you are presented with a set of goods you will be able to respond quickly, rather than having to solve a food puzzle, deciding what to do with each ingredient or studying an unfamiliar method. In short, imagine all potential situations you might face and form a plan of action to deal with each.

CONCLUSION

The CMC level of certification brings with it a stature that only a select few can claim, and is a true measure of the vast store of knowledge and level of skill they have acquired. Though not for everyone, the challenge of trying to achieve CMC status is, itself, highly rewarding; succeeding at it, the icing on the cake.

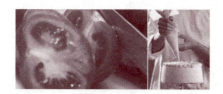

Index

130